VITAL TRUTHS TO

SHAPE YOUR LIFE

VITAL TRUTHS
TO SHAPE YOUR LIFE

STUART BRISCOE

Tyndale House Publishers, Inc.
WHEATON, ILLINOIS

Published in association with the literary agency of
Alive Communications, Inc., 7680 Goddard Street,
Suite 200, Colorado Springs, CO 80920.

Library of Congress Cataloging-in-Publication Data

Briscoe, D. Stuart.
    Vital truths to shape your life / Stuart Briscoe.
      p. cm.
Rev. ed. of: Choices for a lifetime. © 1995.
Includes bibliograhpical references.
    ISBN 0-8423-6016-6 (sc)
    1. Christian ethics. 2. Christian life. 3. Values.
I. Briscoe, D. Stuart. Choices for a lifetime. II. Title.
    BJ1251 .B75 2002
    241—dc21   2002006712
Revised

Printed in the United States of America

08 07 06 05 04 03 02
7   6   5   4   3   2   1

To the congregation of Elmbrook Church, with great gratitude
for the many ways in which they lovingly allowed me to be
their Senior Pastor for thirty years;

To the pastoral team, who served with me with great skill,
good humor, and godly devotion; and

To the Council of Elders, who were wise and
wonderful partners in ministry.

CONTENTS

How Does a Fear of the Lord Affect My Behavior?
Conclusion

PREFACE

*F*or thirty years I served as Senior Pastor of Elmbrook Church in suburban Milwaukee, Wisconsin. During that time I spent countless hours listening to people as they recounted the details of their problems and dilemmas, crushed hopes and shattered lives. I counseled them, prayed with them, and endeavored to assist them in their search for forgiveness, peace, hope, and direction. It is hard for me to imagine a greater privilege than to be invited by a needy person to share their inmost thoughts and deepest longings. My hope has always been to point them to the One in whom grace to live well—in all manner of circumstances—may be found.

Looking back over these many years, however, a couple of things stand out in my mind. First, it was very obvious to me that many of the tragic circumstances people were dealing with were caused by wrong decisions. Sometimes the wrong decisions were made by the people themselves, such as the many young women who found themselves divorced and abandoned in their early thirties having been warned, to no avail, against marrying unwisely. At other times, people suffered severe loss as a result of the bad decisions of others—such as people seriously injured in accidents caused by drunken drivers. It became increasingly apparent that great consequences flow from decisions both small and great. But it was equally obvious that people were looking for help—not only in coping with the consequences of bad decisions, but also in making good decisions. Many of them lacked the ability to see the potential consequences of their decisions; others struggled to articulate any basis in core values upon which their decisions could be made.

And so it was that much of the time I spent counseling people was devoted to exploring the subject of values—what they are, what role they play in decision making, what repercussions they have on life, and (particularly) where we get them! We spent a lot of time discussing how, in our pluralistic society, people derive their value systems from a variety of mutually exclusive sources. We explored the presuppositions and the inevitable conclusions of various value systems, and I impressed upon them the biblical system of values upon which they could base God-honoring decisions.

In countless situations, God was pleased to bring blessing. Some found healing from old wounds; others were delivered from potentially tragic mistakes. Not a few had their lives revolutionized as they made decisions that brought their daily lives into line with the patterns that God has ordained.

In addition to the time spent counseling, a major part of my ministry has been devoted to preaching and teaching. The lessons I have learned in dealing with people's problems on a one-on-one basis have led me to emphasize values and decision making in my teaching. In ministry to missionaries and church leaders around the world, on college campuses, in pastoral preaching in my home church, and in many clubs and business seminars, the subject is of vital interest.

It is out of the conviction that people are looking for help in establishing a system of values upon which they can base sound and wise decisions that this book has been written. Much of the biblical material used in the book is found in the ancient book of Proverbs—a section of Scripture that deals with the principles upon which life is based and the practical application of these principles in daily living.

I am deeply grateful to my friends at Tyndale House Publishers for the opportunity to make this material available to a wider public and, in particular, to my editor, Shawn Harrison, for his incisive thinking, gracious encouragement, godly insights, and professional skills. Special thanks to Ron Beers and Carla Mayer, with whom the project was first discussed; and Rick Christian and Chip MacGregor of Alive Communications, who make good things happen.

I trust that our efforts will lead to avoiding bad decisions, establishing sound values, and the abundant blessing of God on your life.

*F*reedom creates options. Political freedom allows me to vote for the politician whose platform most closely reflects my political opinions—or not to vote at all. Religious freedom allows me to worship at the church, synagogue, mosque, or temple that I believe teaches the truth. Or I am free not to believe anything. Economic freedom allows me to live where I wish, drive what I prefer, travel where I want, wear what I like, associate with whom I choose.

But all these options require me to choose. I cannot simultaneously vote and not vote. It is impossible to worship and not worship at the same time. I may have a problem deciding between living in Hawaii or the Bahamas and be fortunate enough to have a home in both places, but I do have to choose where to be at any one time! "The man who has everything" may have a Mercedes and a Lexus in the garage but he can't drive both at once. Even *he* is governed by decisions!

One might object that there are no options where there is no freedom—that, for instance, a prisoner does not have choices. Natan

Sharansky, a Russian Jew who was incarcerated for almost a decade in Soviet prisons, would not agree. When he was subjected to humiliating strip searches and abuse in the notorious Lefortovo prison, he determined that he would not allow his captors to humiliate him. He believed that he would only be humiliated if he humiliated himself by doing something of which he would ultimately be ashamed. So he decided to pity his tormentors rather than to despise them, to concentrate on his own reactions rather than their actions. Even in Lefortovo, where freedom was in chains, Sharansky was at liberty to choose.

My friend Jean Robinson served as a missionary for forty years in Zaire when it was the Belgian Congo. When she was seventy, she returned to the U.S. and immediately started to struggle with reverse culture shock. She told me that the most difficult adjustment for her was to make decisions, because she was not used to all the choices. On one occasion she was asked by her daughter-in-law to pick up a jar of applesauce from the supermarket. She hadn't seen applesauce in years. When she eventually found the appropriate shelf, she was so overwhelmed by the variety of applesauces on display that she was paralyzed with indecision and after some considerable time burst into tears, grabbed the nearest jar, and fled the scene.

Jean Robinson's decision, while it was traumatic for her, did not have far-reaching consequences. And Sharansky's decision, which impacted on his own well-being, did little to affect anyone else. But sometimes the decisions that people are required to make are so momentous that millions are affected and the course of history is determined.

WINSTON CHURCHILL

In the late 1930s Neville Chamberlain, the British prime minister, believed that Hitler could be appeased. Winston Churchill believed he should be opposed. Eventually Parliament decided that Churchill should replace Chamberlain. As a result England opposed rather than appeased Hitler.

Not long after England declared war, the mighty Wehrmacht rolled over most of western Europe and Hitler and his forces stood on the coast of France less than twenty miles from the practically defenseless United Kingdom. Instead of invading the UK, Hitler, against the advice of his generals, turned eastward and embarked on his ill-fated campaign against the Soviet Union. What if he had decided to attack the United Kingdom, which, alone with the Commonwealth countries and a few remnants of the defeated allies, stood against him? Later Churchill cabled Franklin Delano Roosevelt, asking for help with the well-known words, "Give us the tools and we'll finish the job." Roosevelt, much to the chagrin of many in the Congress, decided to make supplies available to the beleaguered British and the tide of war began to turn. What if Roosevelt had bowed to pressure from Congress?

KARL MARX

Many of the great events of history hang on great decisions made by great leaders. But not all the decisions that change the world appear to be momentous at the time they are made. In 1867 an unknown Russian censor serving the Russian government, which was normally highly suspicious of anything that might be politically subversive, permitted a questionable book to be published and circulated. He said it "was unlikely to find many readers among the general public." The title of the book was *Das Kapital,* the author an angry, penniless German journalist named Karl Marx. The general public may not have read the book, but somebody did—someone named Vladimir Lenin. The result was Communism, a political movement that at one stage held in its iron grip no less than one third of the world's population and dominated a major part of the twentieth century. What if the unknown censor had banned the book?

3

ALEXANDER FLEMING

In the waning days of the nineteenth century, a young boy left the lowlands of Scotland where he had grown up and moved to London to live with three of his brothers, all of whom were studying medicine. He followed them into their chosen profession and decided to study at St. Mary's Hospital because they had the best water polo team! There he came under the influence of the eminent bacteriologist Almoth Wright, concentrated on bacteriology, and one day discovered penicillin. Since that day the world has never been the same. What if Alexander Fleming had not been a good swimmer? What if he had chosen a different medical school?

CHARLES DARWIN

Another young medical student, who hated the sight of blood, spent two miserable years in medical studies at the insistence of his father, a doctor. Eventually his father reluctantly allowed him to transfer to Cambridge to study divinity. But his heart was not in theology either, and when he was invited to sail as a naturalist on a two-year expedition to South America, his father grudgingly gave him permission—at the last minute! So Charles Darwin embarked on the *Beagle* for a voyage which actually lasted five years, ruined his health, and spawned the theory that changed the way the world thinks about just about everything. Michael Denton, a molecular biologist, wrote, "The voyage of the *Beagle* was [therefore] a journey of awesome significance. Its object was to survey Patagonia; its result was to shake the foundations of Western thought."[1] What if Darwin senior had not changed his mind? What if *On the Origin of the Species by Means of Natural Selection; or, the Preservation of Favored Races in the Struggle for Life*—as the resultant book was ponderously titled—had never been written?

It is practically impossible for modern Westerners to envisage a world without Marx, Fleming, and Darwin. Their influence has been immeasurable, and yet it hinged on relatively insignificant decisions.

The Russian censor could have banned the book or allowed it to be published; Alexander Fleming could have applied to any of the twelve teaching hospitals in London; and Dr. Darwin could have said "Yea" or "Nay" to his son's request to sail to South America. They made their decisions and had no idea of the ramifications. The rest, as they say, is history.

Our lives are shaped by our decisions, and it is a rare decision that does not yield repercussions in the lives of others. So what should we incorporate in a healthy decision-making process?

Most of our decisions require little thought and make few demands either on our time or our energy. Whether or not to wear a tie, and if so, a blue one or a red one, certainly will not cause a tremor on the Richter scale of human existence! Whether to eat a bagel or a muffin for breakfast will probably be determined more by habit than anything else. But what of the major decisions that shape our lives and the lives of those who move within the orbit of our influence? What constitutes a good decision? What differentiates a good one from a bad one? How do I determine a right decision from a wrong decision? And what exactly leads to decisions being made, to one option being preferred over another?

The very words *good, bad, right,* and *wrong* immediately introduce the idea of morality into decision making. And when we inquire why we make the decisions we do, the question of motivation appears on the horizon. We cannot overestimate the moral and motivational dimensions of life's decisions.

When Senator Jim Jeffords of Vermont announced in 2001 that he was leaving the Republican Party, the media paid him considerable attention. There is nothing particularly unusual in a politician changing sides, but Jeffords's move was profoundly significant. The senator was elected only six months before to an evenly divided Senate—fifty Democrats, fifty Republicans. Since Vice President Dick Cheney, a Republican, could cast a tie-breaking vote, the leadership of the Senate rested in Republican hands. But then, with Jeffords's move to become an Independent, the split was fifty to forty-nine in the Democrats' favor. So the control of the Senate switched from Republicans to Democrats, committee chairmanships changed hands, and the agenda of the Senate was determined by different criteria. It was a small change, but one with big ramifications.

Senator Jeffords said that his decision had been a difficult one and that he had just endured the most emotional experience of his life. Despite being wooed and cajoled by his Republican colleagues, he decided to make the change. But he was convinced that his decision was the right one. Not surprisingly, not everybody agreed! In fact, polls showed that more than 60 percent of the public believed it to be fundamentally wrong—immoral—for a politician to change parties after being elected to represent the people as a member of that party. In other words, the morality of the decision was questioned.

And so are Jeffords's motivations. He said his decision was a matter of principle. He insisted that he did not leave the Republicans; the party left him. On principle he could not agree with the policies espoused by the party, and his own conscience would not permit him to stay. That might have been true, but other, less charitable explanations are that he got an offer of a better chairmanship from the Democrats, that he was piqued because of a perceived snub from the White House, or that he was angry that the Republicans were going to scrap one of his pet pork-barrel projects that granted Vermont farmers a milk subsidy that no other farmers receive. Did principle motivate the decision? Or was it pride, pique, payback, or power? Who knows? But we do know that issues of *morality* and *motivation* were involved.

Even though most of us will never live in the heady atmosphere of the "corridors of power," we make major decisions that raise questions about our moral reasoning and motives. What is the basis of our system of values? What do we believe about the purpose of life and how it should be lived? How should we treat people? What about decisions relating to work and play, marriage and family, money and possessions? How do we formulate good decisions? How do we know what is the right decision? How do we rectify wrong decisions? How do we cope with the ramifications of bad decisions?

The following chapters will address these and other issues and formulate answers that will serve to help us make good decisions rather than bad ones, better decisions rather than worse ones, and right decisions rather than wrong ones.

THE CRISIS OF VALUES

We may be one of the few societies incapable of passing on its moral teachings to young people. . . . We've forgotten several thousand years of civilization—the great moral, religious, and philosophical traditions.

CHRISTINA HOFF SOMMERS

*T*alk of morality is a little troubling to the sensibilities of some people nowadays. To them the word *morality* creates visions of fanatical Puritans hunting witches and their puritanical modern day counterparts pursuing anyone who might give the vaguest impression that they are having fun. As Thomas Macaulay famously (though inaccurately) said in his *History of England,* "The Puritan hated bear-baiting, not because it gave the bear pain, but because it gave pleasure to the spectators."[2]

Oddly, even those who are most nervous about the introduction of "morality" into life's equation have a finely developed sense of what is morally acceptable. I have never met an agnostic on the subject of morality when it involves a wrong perceived against one's self! Still, while people don't like to talk about morality, many of them seem quite open to a discussion of "values." So let's talk about values as they relate to decisions.

Suppose someone is driving to work on a busy freeway when the car in front of him swerves violently off the road into the median and disappears from sight. The driver of the following vehicle quickly looks at his watch, decides he's going to be late for an important appointment, and steps on the gas. His decision was based on what was of value to him. To put it bluntly, getting to work on time was more important than possibly saving a life. He put more value on his standing in the office than on the person lying in the wreckage. To consider whether his response was "right" or "wrong"—whether he "should" have stopped and whether or not he "ought" to have called for help—would require a system of values, a code of ethics. And it is precisely at this point that many people seem to be having trouble.

WHO CAN RESTORE SOCIETY'S VALUES?

Part of the problem is knowing from where to derive a system of values—a moral base. Not too long ago people talked about looking to the church or the President, the public school teacher or a famous personality. Now people lament that there "aren't any like them around anymore."

There is a lot of truth to this lament. James Patterson and Peter Kim, in their book *The Day America Told the Truth,* conclude after interviewing thousands of people across the country that "at this time America has no leaders and especially, no moral leadership. Americans believe, across the board, that our current political, religious, and business leaders have failed us miserably and completely."[3] To say we have "no moral leadership" is an excessively gloomy overstatement, but there can be little doubt that many of the people from whom we could reasonably expect to receive a clear message on values have not only failed to deliver, but worse, they may have effectively delivered a powerful message about wrong values.

The Church?

Take, for example, Nicols Fox's article entitled, "What Are Our Real Values?"

Who makes the rules these days that determine how our
society is going to work—the code of ethics behind the
laws that determines our values and decides how we
are going to live together in community? It isn't the
churches. It's not so much that their moral leadership
is being ignored as that, to a great extent, they've abdi-
cated the role. Collectively they seem to exude the same
relativism and insecurity about right and wrong as the
rest of us.[4]

Ms. Fox rightly assumes that society should "work," and for that to
happen society needs to maintain certain rules and values. They need
to come from somewhere; apparently, in her opinion and that of
many others, the church has failed to do the job. And the failure can
be attributed to two causes—inconsistency and irrelevance. The
highly publicized moral failures of Christian ministers and the resultant collapse of their ministries has been scandalous, and their glaring
inconsistencies have been confusing. On one occasion I was confronted by angry students who demanded to know after the failure of
a well-known Christian student leader, "Who of your generation can
we trust? We're struggling against the odds on the campuses and you
leaders are engaging in the things we're struggling against." And
while not as damaging as ministerial inconsistency, ecclesiastical irrelevance does nothing to meet the needs for moral direction that society can and should expect.

The humorous story of a young Kentucky preacher illustrates the
point. The young man in question began his ministry on the first
Sunday by preaching against smoking. At the end of the service the
elders came up to him and said, "Young man, you must realize that a
third of your congregation make their money growing tobacco."

"Oh," he said, "I didn't realize that."

They said, "Well, just bear that in mind in the future."

So the next week he preached against drinking. The elders

promptly informed him, "Young man, you have to realize that in this county a third of the people distill whiskey."

"Oh," he said, "I didn't realize that."

"Well, you do now," they responded ominously.

The third week he preached against gambling. The elders said, "Young man, this is Kentucky. A third of your congregation raises thoroughbred racehorses."

"Oh," he said, "I never even thought about that."

So the fourth week, finally getting the message, he preached on the dangers inherent in deep-sea diving in international waters!

The young preacher was quite right in asserting that drinking, smoking, and gambling have negative effects on health and well-being, but he took the way of discretion and limited his remarks to truth that was palatable, politically correct—and irrelevant. Now that may be a smart course of action for a young pastor with job security on his mind, but it does add fuel to the flames of criticism that flicker around the church these days, one of which is that the church has nothing of significance to contribute to the way ordinary people go about their lives.

Politicians?

During the 2001 Washington "intern scandal," Jonathan Alter's comment in *Newsweek* was startling: "For politicians, interns, and reporters, the psychosexual game in the capital will always go on. . . . Adultery is eternal and biological, but in Washington it gets a helping hand."[5] We are confused if adultery is nothing more than a "game" that has existed from eternity and apparently is biological and therefore inevitable, if the behavior of congressmen is not unlike that of donkeys in heat. To date only two congressmen have spoken out about the immorality of this scandal, while hundreds have said nothing, turned away, and looked in the other direction. The general reaction to these two who have spoken up has been that if immorality is grounds for political dismissal, "we'll have to empty the halls of Congress." The public's impression lately has been that we should not expect leadership from politicians, nor even moral rectitude.

The Business Community?

While the business world has finally awakened to the need for moral training after the Wall Street and Enron scandals, one finds some of their approaches to values head-scratching to say the least. Take, for example, the recent column in a publication that describes itself as devoted to "Improving performance through value-centered management." The headline of the column states, "It pays to be ethical with your computer software." Apparently there has been a problem with downsized and fired employees turning in management for software violations such as illegally shared software. As a result guilty companies have been hit with fines totaling many thousands of dollars. So the advice was "purchase all the software your employees need." Why? Because it is the right thing to do? Because it is honest and honesty is a moral principle? No, because it pays. Apparently, for this business publication the highest value resides in the bottom line. And even as the business community pays lip service to values, Congress has opened hearings "on analysts' many conflicts of interest, which in some case are so egregious that even Wall Street has stopped pretending they're all right." The reason for this enquiry is the public exposure of an apparently common practices relating to bankers' kickbacks and analysts' personal gains and insider trading. There's evidently still something rotten even in the state of Wall Street.[6]

The Educational System?

Can we expect more from the educational establishment? A number of years ago I was invited to lunch with the governor of the state in which I live. Apparently he hosted monthly luncheons to which representatives of the life of the state were invited. I represented the religious community! The various representatives of business, law, education, politics, sports, and entertainment were very friendly and gracious, and as we sat down for the meal, I, as the representative of religion, was asked to say grace. I did. A few amens were mumbled and the governor then said, "Let's start with you, Reverend. What do you think we could do to improve the public schools and what they offer to our young people?" I replied, "As I have no personal experience of American education, having been educated in Britain, I am probably not the best person to answer that question. But I would like to suggest that it would be helpful if our young people were taught values." Immediately the atmosphere changed and one Regent of the State University leaned across the table and quite belligerently asked, "Whose values do you want taught? Yours or mine?"

The often-asked question, "Whose values—yours or mine?" has led to a policy attitude that advocates "value-free" or "value-neutral" education: As we can't agree whether we should teach my values or yours, we'll settle for teaching none. The unfortunate result of this approach has been that young people may be led to believe that it is possible to live life value-free—which, in addition to being itself a value, is totally and dangerously wrong.

Stephen Arons, a professor of legal studies at the University of Massachusetts, wrote that public schools have become "bland, homogenized, ethically numb, and assertively mediocre."[7] Notice "ethically numb." How numb?

Christina Hoff Sommers, after teaching ethics at the university level for fifteen years, was convinced that there was something fundamentally wrong in the American classroom. She wrote, "We may be one of the few societies incapable of passing on its moral teachings to young people." She went on to say that when it comes to moral education it is as if "we've forgotten several thousand years of civilization—the great moral, religious, and philosophical traditions."[8]

It's not that our educators are unmindful of the need for character development in our younger generation. Their difficulties seem to arise from an almost religious zeal to protect the state from invasion by the church, and a corresponding enthusiasm for scrupulously avoiding any form of moral teaching that could be a kind of "brainwashing."

Many educators seem to have arrived at a strange compromise: to teach something called social morality without the embarrassment of having to teach private morality—as if the two can be successfully divorced. This, as Dr. Sommers pointed out, allows students to "debate abortion, euthanasia, capital punishment, DNA research, and the ethics of transplant surgery while they learn almost nothing about private decency, honesty, personal responsibility, or honor."[9]

The Media?

To whom can we turn for help? Which of our remaining great institutions can come to the aid of a society that acknowledges the deterioration of its culture?

Why not the media? After all, this is the age of multimedia—it hits us at every turn—and no one knows the full extent to which we are affected by the messages conveyed through the media. Of course, if the millions of dollars spent annually in advertising are any indication, savvy business people believe in the power of media to affect behavior. Can we expect any help in instilling solid values from the entertainment media?

Lisa Schwarzbaum, in an article for *Entertainment Weekly,* wrote about the "filth, raunch, violence, and hate" that dominate popular culture.[10] Eminem's brand of hate, misogyny, homophobia, scatology, and violence continues to fill the airwaves. The downward trend is clearly evidenced by the "aging" Madonna being outflanked in the outrage department by younger stars, while Howard Stern, the bottom feeder in the fish tank of celebrity, loses ground to newcomers Opie and Anthony, whose brand of broadcasting has descended even deeper into the murk. Meanwhile, MTV has captured the music market and the hearts and minds of millions of teenagers playing such masterpieces as "I Wanna Be Bad" by Willa Ford and by broadcasting the material of such groups as Public Enemy and Badly Drawn Boy whose chosen names say all that needs to be said about their moral outlook. No wonder Sir David Frost once described television as a medium that allows you to invite into your den someone you would not allow in your home.

Some people are asking an honest question: If this is so, why do we still watch the movies and listen to the music? Could it be that there is a kind of schizophrenia at work here, whereby the higher, nobler part of us desires the values, and the lower, ignoble part responds to the countervalues it outwardly deplores? Nicols Fox seems to think so:

> The trouble is, real American values are expressed not by what we say we wish for, but by what we really do. . . . Perhaps the best indicator of what we really are is what we spend our money on or what we watch on television. Look at what we read. Look at what we choose to do with our spare time. That's what we value.[11]

We're getting a clear picture here. There is general consensus that our society is in trouble, that our culture is wearing thin. Commentators from the right and the left at last agree on something! The problem appears to be related to a lack of core values or beliefs that will affect behavior in a positive way. But who is to teach these principles? The various opinions suggest that the church doesn't teach them, media won't teach them, education can't teach them, and politics dare not teach them. So where do we go from here?

POVERTY OF VALUES, LACK OF MODELS
Let's go to southern California. The year was 1992, and Vice President Dan Quayle was addressing the faithful in what turned out to be an

MiFinca

422 East Mountain Pkwy.
Salyersville

COUPON

Get 25%
Off any individual meal
with this coupon!!

unsuccessful attempt to get reelected. In his speech he made a connection between the recent terrifying rioting in Los Angeles and what he called a "poverty of values." During the course of his speech, he also made a brief reference to Murphy Brown, a popular TV character played on a weeknight sitcom by the accomplished actress Candice Bergen. Murphy Brown, a single, bright, articulate woman, had gotten pregnant. The American viewing public held its collective breath, waiting for the arrival of the baby! Would it be a boy or a girl? Apparently the illegitimacy of the baby's birth and the problems attached to single parenthood were lost on the American consciousness. Vice President Quayle made a brief comment in his speech that this was another illustration of the poverty of values afflicting the culture.

Immediately an immense furor developed. Johnny Carson, soon to retire, thanked Mr Quayle for "coming through" for him again, while David Letterman weighed in with, "Mr. Vice President, I don't know how to tell you this, but Murphy Brown is a fictional character." Feminists of various stripes expressed outrage that the vice president should be so insensitive to the lot of many brave, self-sacrificing single moms, pointing out the inherent nobility of Murphy's action in that she did not abort the child but selflessly went ahead with the confinement and was now embarking on the difficult and often thankless task of raising the child on her own. The talk shows, the call-in shows, the editorial writers, and the politicians, not to mention the preachers, jumped on the bandwagon—and the ratings of Murphy Brown went into the stratosphere. Suddenly the whole issue of values was front and center.

While this was happening, *Newsweek* ran a cover story written by Joe Klein, a senior editor, in which he stated, "Flawed vehicle though he may be, Dan Quayle seems to have nudged presidential politics perilously close to something that really matters: a debate on values and the American family."[12] Now, isn't it sad that in a debate on something as significant and profound as values, the proponents found it necessary to utilize fictional models, created by the media, to make their points? Maybe we are not only suffering from a poverty of values but also a poverty of models. Can't we do better than that?

"I BELIEVE IN . . . THE CHURCH"

While the criticisms leveled at the church by people like Nicols Fox do have some validity, in order to be fair, we must give consideration to another side of the issue. The fact is, the church is making a positive impact on communities. In some segments of our society, the church is the only institution having any kind of effect on values. Recently I was told by a sociologist working in some of the most troubled major cities in America that, in his experience, the church was the only institution that was holding together some dangerous areas of the cities.

Many people in our society are looking for someone to give them a clear lead. They are troubled by the way the society is going but confused by the cacophony of voices shouting conflicting messages.

A few days ago a fashionably dressed woman came to me at the end of one of our Sunday services and said, "This is the first time I've been in this church. My friend was accepted into membership today and I came to witness the event. I greatly enjoyed the music, the prayers were moving, and the sermon was stimulating. It was a wonderful experience. But something bothers me."

I encouraged her to tell me what was on her mind.

She went on. "I've heard that this church does not accept some people. Can that be true?"

"What kind of people?" I enquired.

"Well, gays and lesbians and people like that. I've heard you won't accept them."

"That depends on what you understand by accepting people," I replied. "Let me give you an example. If you have a teenaged son who goes into the drug scene, engages in petty crime, and ends up in jail would you still accept him as your son?"

"Of course I would," she replied.

"But would you accept his behavior?" I asked.

"Absolutely not," she said without hesitation.

"Then am I right in saying you would accept his personhood but not his actions?"

"Absolutely," she concurred.

"Then let me explain our position as far as gays and lesbians are concerned. We regard them as infinitely precious people created by God and loved by Christ and by us. We accept them as profoundly significant people. But we cannot accept their lifestyle for a very simple reason: We do not believe it can be characterized as normative, which is what they want us to do."

"Why not?' she queried.

"Because Scripture says, 'From the beginning of creation God created male and female and for this reason a man will leave his father and mother and be joined to his wife and they shall become one flesh.' That is a creation principle, which in modern day language says, in effect, that God invented sex and sexuality, and he outlined the social environment in which it should be practiced and enjoyed. That environment is heterosexual, monogamous marriage. Any sexual activity of any kind outside of those divinely established limits is abnormal and unacceptable."

Her immediate response surprised me. "That makes perfect sense. Thank you. I never knew what I believed myself until you explained the situation."

Now I'm not suggesting that everyone will be so readily convinced, but I am saying that reasonable people are open to hear what someone who believes something has to say if it is backed with grace and consistency. This is the church's opportunity.

A couple of years ago, our church went through deep waters when charges were leveled against one of our youth pastors, which led to his committing suicide. Imagine the trauma as this shocking event suddenly hit the congregation with the force of a spiritual tornado. Then multiply the impact a hundredfold when the police took over and the media descended upon the church and the issue became the talk of the city. The congregation, although deeply distressed, responded to the authorities and the media with grace and consideration, coupled with frankness and courtesy. They were asked hard questions, and they gave honest answers. The end result was people walking in off the street and asking for help, telling of problems for which they had sought answers for decades. The local newspaper—not known primarily as an advocate of evangelical Christianity—concluded their coverage with an editorial entitled, in bold letters, "Elmbrook Church Got It Right." They complimented the church on believing something firmly and acting consistently in such a way as to give a lead to the society as a whole.

It is unlikely that a lot of help will be coming from educators, the media, or the politicians. Perhaps we can be more hopeful about the church. Perhaps God's people can speak out winsomely and compellingly and cast some sweetness and light on the troubled waters of our culture's values. But what exactly does the church have to say on the subject? How well is it being said? And is anybody listening? These are the questions we can explore together in the chapters to come.

What democracy needs is a value system that legitimizes
both individual rights and social authority
and establishes a balance between the two.

A. JAMES REICHLEY

I once spoke to a group of missionaries in a conference center on the outskirts of Brasília, the capital of Brazil. After the final session, a group of conferees went down to the snack bar, where one of the veteran missionaries insisted on buying everyone ice cream and a local drink called *guaraná*. He fished an immense bundle of cruzeiros, the Brazilian currency, from his pocket and said with a laugh, "I may as well spend these things because at the present rate of inflation they will have little or no value in the morning."

A similar thing happened in Germany many years ago when the reichsmark became valueless and the deutschemark took its place. I remember a young girl, a member of a party I was leading to Germany, showing me a fistful of money she had brought to spend on her vacation. When I inquired where she got it, she told me her father had saved it up from the days when he served in the army in Germany during World War II. Unfortunately for her, she held in her hand bundles of worthless reichsmarks. They had no value. They could be exchanged for nothing of significance.

The debate over values is more than a discussion of declining currencies, or even economies. What exactly do we mean by values? Values are the basis of the decisions that change our lives and the lives of others, so this is a question that needs to be answered with great care.

DISCOVERING WHAT OUR VALUES ARE

Hunter Lewis, in *A Question of Values,* defines values as "personal beliefs that propel us to action, to a particular kind of behavior and life."[13]

These beliefs can be held with varying degrees of intensity and thus vary dramatically in the impact they make on behavioral patterns. Lewis suggests, for instance, that beliefs, in ascending order of intensity, may be demonstrated by interests, preferences, respect, and commitment. Let me illustrate.

If I work from the age-old premise that "you can always find time to do what you really want to do," then the way you spend your leisure time will be a good indicator of your interests and values. If you prefer functioning as a "couch potato" rather than training for a marathon, it is reasonable to conclude that you do not value physical fitness highly. Or if you prefer spending leisure time with your grandchildren rather than playing golf, then it would probably be correct to assume that you highly value the extended family. Your interests help identify your values.

If you were awakened in the middle of the night by the blare of a fire alarm, and you had minutes to escape the blazing building, what would you grab first? You wouldn't be able to take everything, so you would have to choose between one thing and another. It might require choosing between the cat and the children's photos, the family Bible and the autographed baseball. Which way would you go? What you chose, all things being equal, would indicate your preferences and thus your values.

But we can go further. Ask yourself, *What is it that I treasure so highly that I am irritated when other people ignore it?* What are the things I respect so deeply that I tend to be resentful of those who treat them with disrespect? Recently, one of our elderly ushers was incensed when a young man came into church and sat in the pew with a baseball cap on his head—backwards! The usher asked me what he should do, and by the look on his face he appeared to be debating whether to take the cap off the head or the head off the shoulders! He was irritated by what appeared to be a total lack of respect for something he valued highly. Good, old-time courtesy was high on his list of values, and his irritation for those who did not share his views loudly declared it.

Deeply held beliefs turn into fiercely defended commitments. Things worth living for become things worth dying for. When the Founding Fathers of the United States made their historic decision to sign the Declaration of Independence in 1776, they pledged "our lives, our fortunes, and our sacred honor." This was not grandiose rhetoric. They were liable to be charged with treason, and they could easily have lost their livelihoods and their very lives. But from their perspective, they had to take the risk, because what they believed about liberty was significant enough to demand ultimate commitment. There was no doubt about what they valued.

Revolutions and burning homes are not the stuff of normal, daily life, but they illustrate how we can get in touch with the values we hold. We often go through life barely conscious of what we value. But to deal with situations both extreme and mundane, we should identify and think about them.

HOW DO WE LEARN VALUES?

Values are more than preferences or interests. They are beliefs that produce in us a commitment. That commitment is so significant that it leads us to decide and behave in a certain way, and our behavior establishes a lifestyle. So our value-driven decisions build a life.

Values incorporate a moral component into the people we are and the lives we live. At the personal level, values determine the character of the person we meet on the street; at the societal level, values decide the kind of street on which we meet that person. I may meet a mugger or a merchant on the street; that person's values will determine which they are. The street may be a tree-lined haven where children play contentedly or a burned-out shell of a neighborhood where drug traffickers wage war with automatic weapons; the values of my society and neighborhood will decide which it will be.

But how can values vary so drastically? How can people believe so differently? How can neighborhoods differ so dramatically?

One reason is that we learn about life differently. Our background, environment, and upbringing have a role in how we view life. Hunter Lewis suggests six sources for our values:

- Authority
- Deductive logic
- Sensory experience
- Emotion
- Intuition
- Science[14]

To illustrate how these ways of learning might play out, let's take the situation of a woman discovering she's pregnant. In a culture where abortion is both legal and controversial, she must process widely divergent opinions on the subject. But abortion is at least a hypothetical option for her as she ponders the new life in her womb. The following instances illustrate how we process information in different ways and thus arrive at decisions that affect our lives and the lives of others.

Authority
One woman—raised in a Catholic home, educated in parochial school, and devoted to her church—accepts the pope's authority. He, speaking for the church, has announced that abortion is wrong. Be-

cause she has a high regard for his authority, she decides not to have an abortion. Another woman, raised in a totally secular environment, has no interest in what the pope or the church says but because the Supreme Court, which wields great authority, has said abortion is legal, she accepts that authority and has the abortion. They accept different sources of authority and therefore arrive at opposite conclusions.

Deductive Logic

Another woman, discovering that she is unexpectedly and unhappily pregnant, immediately worries about herself and what the pregnancy will mean to her personal life. Her friends tell her to abort the child but she argues that killing is wrong, that abortion is killing, and therefore, abortion is wrong. And on the basis of that line of reasoning, she decides to carry the child to term. But another argues that the embryo is part of the woman's body, the woman has the right to determine what happens to her own body, and therefore, abortion is permissible. Accordingly she terminates the pregnancy. Both argue on the basis of deductive logic, but starting with different premises leads them to opposite conclusions.

Sensory Experience

While I recognize that I as a man have no idea what pregnancy and delivery of a child feel like, I have met a number of women who in the course of counseling have talked about the discomfort and the pain of childbearing on the one hand, and the joy and delight of holding a newborn baby on the other. I have no difficulty imagining both to be true. But if a woman makes decisions on the basis of her feelings, she might easily be swayed by the discomfort and pain and decide not to have the child, while another will decide that these dimensions of motherhood are irrelevant when compared to the joy of holding the baby. Both decide on the basis of feelings—of sensory experience.

Emotion

Postpartum depression gets a lot of publicity in the mercifully rare event of a mother murdering her children. But it happens. Here again, men cannot talk with any degree of personal knowledge about this kind of depression, and it can never be made an excuse for murder. But it is possible that some women who have experienced it may decide, purely on the basis of their fear, not to bring their pregnancy to term, while other women have felt so alive and healthy and energetic during previous pregnancies that they welcome the unborn child with delight and cannot wait for the thrill of bringing up the child. Emotions, too, can lead to entirely different decisions.

Intuition

Female intuition is legendary. How it works and what it is I cannot say. But having lived with my wife for more than forty-three years, I am a firm believer in it! If a woman's decisions are driven solely by intuition, different possibilities present themselves in the case of a pregnancy. One woman may intuit that this will be a great and wonderful experience, that she will greatly benefit from it, that the child she will bear will be a source of endless delight. She will have the baby. Her friend down the street, however, has premonitions of doom and gloom, of trouble and hardship. Rather than face what she is convinced will be a bad experience, she decides on an abortion. On pure intuition they arrive at opposite ends of the issue.

Science

We are all aware that whenever a scientific study is cited to prove that women who have abortions are susceptible to post-abortion guilt feelings, there is always a contradictory "latest" study proving conclusively that the incidence of depression is no greater among women who have abortions than it is for women who suffer postpartum depression. But let's suppose that two pregnant women read the latest scientific journals. One reads about the guilt feelings and shies away from an abortion, and the other reads that there is no more possibility of depression if she has an abortion than if she does not. So using exactly the same method, one decides one way and one the other.

Remember, these examples simply serve to point out one reason that there are so many differing value systems.

The Word of God

I was raised in a God-fearing family where the Word of God was regarded as the final authority in matters of faith and practice. My parents believed that children should be seen and not heard, wash their own dishes, clean their own shoes, and not answer back. This early training made it relatively easy for me to accept the rigorous discipline of the Royal Marines in later life. It almost seemed like a relief at times! As a result I learned to accept authority, and I have never ceased to respect it and learn from it.

But a six-year-old child whose father walks out on the family and takes up with another woman while refusing to pay child support, thus banishing the child and his mother to intense financial and emotional strain, will probably have great difficulty accepting authority and trusting people. He or she would be more likely to learn distrust of authority from bitter emotions and painful experience.

Our learning and believing are affected not only by background but also by our assumptions and presuppositions. We normally say, for example, that seeing is believing, when in actual fact the opposite is nearer the truth—believing is seeing. When the disciples saw the Lord walking toward them on the stormy waters of Galilee, they believed it was a ghost. Why? Because they believed in ghosts but not people walking on water! So all the evidence to the contrary, they believed they saw a ghost, when what they were seeing but not believing was the Lord of creation demonstrating his power.

In our lives, as well, we more often respond according to what we know than what we haven't yet discovered. And sometimes what we know is not quite true or not completely true—or false altogether—while what we have yet to discover could be the very principle that will save us from self-destruction.

THREE POSSIBLE FOUNDATIONS FOR OUR BELIEFS

Let's say that all of us have received information from a variety of sources—our different backgrounds and different means of getting knowledge about life. What do we do with this information? How do we decide and what do we determine? There are three entirely different ways of doing this based on three totally different presuppositions. The suppositions can be stated as follows:

1. The autonomous self has the sole right and responsibility to decide.
2. The society of which I am a part determines the way to go.
3. The sovereign Lord has the right to direct and govern my thinking and my deciding.

Self Determines What Is True and Right

This is a common supposition today: Nobody else has the right or the ability to choose for the autonomous self. It is "none of their business." So every person is responsible to come to his or her own conclusions and ignore what everyone else says or thinks about them. Jerry Rubin, co-founder of the "yippie" (Youth International Party) movement, said that the liberated man "can do what he wants whenever he wants to do it." I once heard a man sitting behind me at a baseball game announce, "Ain't nobody gonna to tell me nothin' no way." On the basis of his excruciating abuse of the English language I doubt if he had ever heard of "autonomous," but he certainly understood the concept. A well-known rock star once proudly said, "I can go where I want, do what I want, say what I want. There are no rules. Freedom's just another word for a mess someone else has to clean up." That's the self taking charge and calling the shots! Apparently the irony of stating "there are no rules" while postulating self-determined rules of freedom bordering on anarchy escaped this liberated gentleman!

W. E. Henley in his famous poem "Invictus" put it less crudely but no less forcefully:

> *In the fell clutch of circumstance,*
> *I have not winged nor cried aloud.*
> *Under the bludgeonings of chance*
> *my head is bloody, but unbowed.*
> *Beyond this place of wrath and tears*
> *looms but the horror of the shade,*
> *and yet the menace of the years*
> *finds, and shall find, me unafraid.*
> *It matters not how strait the gate,*
> *how charged with punishments the scroll,*
> *I am the master of my fate;*
> *I am the captain of my soul.*[15]

Woody Allen, the filmmaker, had a much publicized live-in arrangement with actress Mia Farrow. Ms. Farrow, as a result of various marriages, liaisons, and adoptions, had amassed quite a large "family" of children for whom Woody Allen functioned in a somewhat ambiguous manner as a father figure. That is, until it was discovered that he was having an affair with one of the children, a teenager. Even hard-boiled, scandal-calloused New Yorkers thought this was going too far and said so. Mr. Allen was unhappy with the bad publicity he received, and when challenged by a reporter as to why he would do such a thing, he answered rather truculently, "The heart wants what it wants." This implies that the autonomous self determines what it wants and goes for it without taking anything else into consideration, including the need to explain itself to other people. It takes but a moment's thought to recognize that a society operating on such a principle will inevitably fracture and fragment. Freedom is a precious thing. People have died to procure it. America was founded upon it. But the unrestrained, ungoverned, unrestricted freedom advocated by those who worship at the shrine of autonomy leads not to liberty but to anarchy.

Society Determines What Is True and Right

This approach at least acknowledges that the individual cannot go it alone and that society cannot survive when made up of people intent on doing their own thing. Of course, some societies have become so authoritarian that they ignore and even abuse the individuals under their care. The polar opposite of unrestrained individual freedom is unrelieved societal domination, in which people are denied the opportunity to travel where they wish, worship as they desire, say what they believe, and assemble with those to whom they relate. All attempts to restrain unrestrained personal behavior must stop far short of such draconian methods. A. James Reichley had this in mind when he insisted, "What democracy needs is a value system that legitimizes both individual rights and social authority and establishes a balance between the two."[16]

But there are still problems when society becomes the determining factor in values. We saw this clearly when the U.S. Supreme Court decided to hear a case dealing with pornography. One of the justices was quite frank about his own dilemma, saying that he had difficulty defining pornography—but he knew it when he saw it! It was hardly surprising, therefore, when the Court came to the conclusion that pornography is that which offends local community standards. Notice "local" community standards. This got them off the hook but impaled just about everybody else. They were operating on the assumption that what would make the hair stand on end in Peoria, Illinois, would not even raise an eyebrow in San Francisco, California. So much for society deciding values! Obviously this approach raises more questions than it provides answers. Which society? Or, more accurately, which segment of society? The majority? The special interest groups? The most vocal? The most powerful? The people with money? The media?

There are those who profess a kind of reverence for the common sense of the American people and their innate ability to know what is right. Politicians are often heard to intone such platitudes when they hope that this infallible populace will be commonsensical enough to vote for them! But Carl Bernstein of Watergate fame is not as impressed:

> We are in the process of creating, in sum, what deserves to be called the idiot culture. Not an idiot subculture, which every society has bubbling beneath the surface and which can provide harmless fun, but the culture itself. For the first time in our history the weird and the stupid and the coarse are becoming our cultural norm, even our cultural ideal.[17]

So, given that society is made up of widely—and wildly—divergent people with special interests, idiosyncrasies, and even idiotic ideals, should we accept that society should be the sole determinant of values? I think not!

The Sovereign Lord Determines What Is True and Right

The third possible approach to a value system is that there is a sovereign Lord from whom we come, through whom we live, by whom we survive, and to whom we are accountable. And he is himself the source of all that is of value. It is in his being—his character and will and purpose—that those things that are good and right and true are to be found, and he has revealed himself and all his values to us in his Son, Jesus Christ, and in Scripture. So it is in relationship to this sovereign Lord that we find our system of values. It is through the spiritual life this Son gives us and through the ministry of the Holy Spirit that we can gain insight into these values, as well as obtain the power to put them into practice.

Almost three quarters of Americans (72 percent) strongly believe in God as the "all-powerful, all-knowing, perfect creator of the universe who rules the world today."[18] So with approximately 72 percent of the American population being "believers," to a greater or lesser extent, we could reasonably conclude that the dominant lifestyle in America is godly, devout, and morally upright. But if visitors from outer space arrived in America, I doubt very much they would recognize godliness, devotion, and moral rectitude. So what's the problem? Why, if the population is made up primarily of believers in an all-powerful and perfect God who created and rules over the universe, is the culture so impregnated with behaviors that are contrary to all that this God is? Let me try to answer that question.

BELIEVING IN GOD

Isaiah the prophet, speaking earnestly to the troubled city of Jerusalem, told the people, "And so the Lord says, 'These people say they are mine. They honor me with their lips. but their hearts are far away'" (Isa. 29:13, NLT). A little more than 700 years later Jesus echoed those sentiments to the descendants of Isaiah's audience, who had apparently not learned from the disastrous consequences of their ancestors' ambivalence towards God. " So why," he said, " do you call me Lord when you won't obey me. Anyone who listens and doesn't obey is like a person who builds a house without a foundation. When the floods sweep down against that house, it will crumble into a heap of ruins" (Luke 6:46, 49, NLT). In Isaiah's time lips and heart were out of synch; in Jesus' time obeisance and obedience were out of step. But why?

Many years ago I knew a small boy called Malcolm. One Sunday morning Malcolm was playing on the carpet with his toy train. The radio broadcast of the Anglican service of morning prayer was playing quietly in the background. On the surface Malcolm was not paying any attention to the service. When the vicar with sonorous tones began to intone the words of the Apostles' Creed. . . .—"I believe in God"—Malcolm, without looking up or in any way deviating from his play, replied in a childlike version of the sonorous tones, "So do I," and carried on playing with his toys.

Sadly there is a grave possibility that we humans can "believe in God" without it making any discernible difference in our lives. We can be thoroughly orthodox in our creedal affirmations without allowing the enormity of our professions or belief to affect our lifestyles in any way. We can say with Malcolm, "So do I," and carry on playing with our toys—more sophisticated than Malcolm's—as if we had said nothing more significant than "I believe in the tooth fairy."

What Does It Mean Truly to Believe in God?

A friend of mine was challenged about his faith by a young student who said, "I don't believe in God." My friend replied, "Tell me about the God you don't believe in because I probably don't believe in him either!" Good point! To say "I believe in God" or conversely "I don't believe in God" without in any way specifying the nature, character, purposes, and intentions of this God is to say nothing of significance. When questioned about "God" many people betray a tendency to reverse one of the most fundamental principles of Scripture. Genesis 1: 26 (NLT) records God saying, "Let us make people in our image, to be like ourselves," while the modern tendency is for people to say, "Let us make God in our image, to be like ourselves." I've never heard anybody say that was what they were doing, but I've heard countless people say, "I could never believe in a God who would do so-and-so," the "so-and-so" in question being something that the Bible specifically says that God has every intention of doing! The result? We have people who believe in a God portrayed in the Bible as long as that portrayal does not infringe on their preconceptions about God or require them to revise their preferences about life. One young man told me in all seriousness that what the Bible says about sexual behavior is perfectly right but totally impractical for the modern era. He concluded, therefore, that what God said about sexual behavior, while it was the correct way to go, did not apply to him! So he was not only remaking God in his image, but he was also reforming God's will to his liking.

Who God Really Is

So how do we come to the point of wanting to do it God's way rather than ours? By coming to the realization of who God really is. And the only way we can do that is by giving careful attention to his self-revelation in Christ and in Scripture. In the Old Testament we have a lengthy presentation of the way God related to his chosen people, the Jews. This is how God revealed himself to them. He took initiative and established a covenant with them, in which he promised to be their God, to lead them, guide them, provide for them, redeem them from their enemies, and bring them into a land of plenty. This action on God's part was not in any way prompted by the exemplary behavior or the innate superiority of the Jewish people, but arose purely from his love, grace, and eternal purposes, which were based on his nature and character. In response the chosen people were to love, honor, respect, worship, and obey the Lord. They were expected to live in loving gratitude and obedience, but loving, trusting obedience does not come naturally to Adam's sinful children! That is why the Old Testament is one long saga of disobedience and disappointment, repentance and restoration, faithlessness and forgiveness. But God persevered with his people, and one day he sent the Messiah he had promised them.

When Jesus came he lived in obscurity for thirty years and in the public eye for three. But those three years changed the world! He showed people what the invisible God is really like and demonstrated a hatred of sin and a love for sinners that knew no bounds. In fact, this love and hatred were two sides of the same coin—the sin he hated was responsible for the abuse of the sinners he loved. His expression of hatred for that which had ruined his creation was a demonstration of love for what was no longer pristine as he intended.

The critical consequence of sin—rebellion against God's laws—is death. Death preceded by disease and despair, disappointment and disintegration, discomfort and disaster, dysfunction and disjunction—everything that has made God's world hellish. But in his death on the cross, Jesus absorbed all these consequences of sin and the judgment of the Holy God against sin. In rising again from the dead, Jesus showed not only that he had conquered death but also that he had satisfied all the demands of God against a sinful race. He made it possible for men and women to be forgiven and introduced to a new life characterized by the very love, honor, respect, worship, and obedience that they were previously incapable of showing. Jesus did this not because he was impressed by our moral superiority or exemplary behavior, but out of his own love and grace.

The Big Decision

There is a consistency in Scripture from Genesis to Revelation—a consistency that shows God loving people, providing for them out of grace, and requiring them to decide to receive his blessings with loving obedience and trusting faith.

A monumental decision is required. And it is this decision that is the key to all the other decisions that will change your life. It is a decision to accept grace's gift of salvation by faith and to live out of gratitude as a devoted follower of the risen Lord in the power of his indwelling Spirit. It is a decision to really believe in God—the God revealed in Christ and Scripture.

Someone will object at this point and say, "I don't think you should emphasize our decision to accept God's gracious offer of salvation in

Christ. Surely the big decision was God's—a decision to accept us!" I think we should balance both. It was clearly God's decision to create us in the first place that started the whole saga. It was his decision not to destroy us after the rebellion—the Fall, as it is called—that meant we survived as a race. It was his decision to offer salvation through Christ, and it was his decision to send Christ into the world, to accept his sacrifice, and to raise him from the dead as evidence of that acceptance that made salvation available. It is his decision to send the Holy Spirit to prompt us to begin to seek after him that is crucial. Of course the initiative is with him. But he treats us as responsible people and requires us to choose to follow him.

Jesus came to the Galilean fishermen and said, "'Come, be my disciples, and I will show you how to fish for people.' And they left their nets at once and went with him" (Matt. 4:19-20, NLT). Later, when Peter preached the first Christian sermon, the people were deeply moved by his statement, "God has made this Jesus whom you crucified to be both Lord and Messiah!" Their response was, "What should we do" to which Peter replied, "Each of you must turn from your sins and turn to God, and be baptized in the name of Jesus. . . . Those who believed what Peter said were baptized and added to the church" (Acts 2:36-41, NLT). In other words they were presented with the challenge to decide whether or not they would believe in the God and Father of our Lord Jesus Christ, turn from their sin, accept his forgiveness, and live in newness of life through his Spirit. They considered the challenge and decided.

The greatest decision that can ever be made is the decision to respond to God's self-revelation, to worship and honor him as he is rather than how we would like him to be, and in so doing to embark on a lifestyle predicated on loving, trusting obedience. The follower of Jesus, having made this decision, desires to know more and more of God's purposes and plans. The one who believes learns them from careful study of Scripture and from commitment to the fellowship of believers where nurture and encouragement in godly living can be found. For the believer, the decisions of life will not be made on the basis of what the autonomous self desires, nor even what the society endorses, but on what the Lord wills.

So let me ask you a personal question. Like everybody else you have adopted a lifestyle. But now you recognize that behind every lifestyle lies a set of values, and these values have prompted the decisions you have made and continue to make about life. Now the question is, "From what source do your values come?" They need to come from the Lord. That means committing your life to him, trusting him, and living in obedience to him.

FINDING TRUTH

If you don't know where you're going, you may end up someplace else.

YOGI BERRA

The story is told of the brash young man who came screeching to a halt at the crossroads in his shiny sportscar. He shouted to an old countryman sitting outside a pub drinking a glass of ale, "I say, old man, can you tell me the way to London?"

"'Fraid I can't, young fella," he replied.

"Well, how far is it to St. Albans?"

"Couldn't tell you that for sure, either."

"You don't know much, do you?" the young man said in exasperation.

"You're right there, young fella. But I'm not lost."

The old timer didn't know much but he knew where he was. The young man thought he knew a lot, but he didn't know where he was, and he had no idea how to get where he was going! He was lost. In practical terms, he was at the crossroads. He had to make a decision and he did not know what he needed to know to make it. This young man was about to prove Yogi Berra right one more time!

A STEP IN THE RIGHT DIRECTION

The information that is so vital to the making of good decisions must be true. That is a tall order! There is no shortage of information available—after all this is the Information Age! The remarkable sophistication in modern communication means that no stone is left unturned in an effort to make information available and understandable. And with how-to books filling the shelves of bookstores, there should be no problem in getting practical advice. Modern studies in human behavior concentrate on making the information both practical and relevant. So all should be well, right? Not necessarily! The critical ingredient in all information is truth. Without truth, everything else—practicality, relevance, understandability, and doability—may be in place but it will be in the wrong place.

Recently my wife and I flew from Moscow to Irkutsk in Siberia. We knew how long the flight was and when the Aeroflot plane was due to arrive. So through the long, uncomfortable night flight we watched for dawn and kept an eye on our watches. Eventually, after the stipulated five and a half hours, an indecipherable message was broadcast over a barely operational speaker system, the plane landed, and we disembarked. We looked for our friends who had promised to meet us, but they were nowhere to be seen. We looked for our bags, but they too were not in evidence. We noticed that nobody was met by anybody and no transport to anywhere seemed to be available. But we'd heard about Russia and decided that this was how things operated there! So we did what everybody else was doing: We bought some coffee and waited for something to happen. Nothing did! After two hours I met a man who could speak German and learned from him that we had been diverted. We were not in Irkutsk but in a city 400 kilometers away, and we would continue our journey when the fog cleared at our destination.

Our problem was simple and basic. We were believing a misapprehension, building our conclusion on misinformation and coming, therefore, with every good intention, to a totally erroneous conclusion. We assumed we were where we weren't, that our friends were where they weren't, and that our journey would end when it wouldn't. In fact, because we were believing earnestly in that which was incorrect, we had gotten everything wrong. It is one thing to believe—but the sad truth is that you can fervently believe something that is not true. The key ingredient must be truth.

With regard to values, is there such a thing as truth? If so, where is it to be found? Yes, there is truth that can be known, and it is to be found in God's revelation of himself and his purposes in the written Word of God, illustrated in the life of the living Word of God—Jesus. Solid decisions, therefore, need to based on what God has revealed in Christ and in Scripture.

But that answer is not good enough for many people today. In their minds, Scripture is, at best, a mildly interesting book that is virtually incomprehensible; at worst, it is an antiquated book full of irrelevant ideas and outmoded information. In fact, it would never occur to them to refer to the Bible for practical help in making the basic decisions of life. But this is unfortunate, because the Bible is an essentially practical book that is readily understandable to anyone who will approach it with an open mind and a sense of expectation and desire.

THE WAY OF WISDOM

Let me show you the practical side of the Bible. One of the main sections of the Old Testament is called "wisdom literature" because *wisdom* is one of the dominant themes. This Hebrew word for "wisdom" has interesting connotations. The old craftsmen who worked long and hard on the tabernacle's intricate furnishings, according to the instructions given by the Lord to Moses, were recognized as having received special "skill" from the Lord (Exod. 31:6, NLT). In Psalm 107 the psalmist graphically portrays the terror of sailors caught in a storm where they are "at their wits' end" (Ps. 107:27, NLT). And in

1 Kings 3:9 we are told about the humble request of Solomon, who, realizing the immensity of the task God had given him, asked that he might be given "a discerning heart . . . to distinguish between right and wrong." In each of these examples the word used to describe the special skills of craftsmen, sailors, and king is closely related to the word for wisdom. In its original usage the word simply meant "skill," but with the passage of time it broadened to mean "skill in living." So William E. Mouser Jr. defines wisdom as "The practical skills to live successfully and the moral discipline to learn and implement those skills."[19]

In the Hebrew community, with its unique relationship to God, skillful living was synonymous with living by the standards of the covenant, as outlined by the Lord. So Allen P. Ross writes in the *Expositor's Bible Commentary*:

> In the book of Proverbs "wisdom" signifies skillful living—the ability to make wise choices and live successfully according to the moral standards of the covenant community. The one who lives skillfully produces things of lasting value to God and the community.[20]

Wisdom in the ancient writings of the people of God amounted to understanding the Lord's principles in order to live wisely and well. It was all about skillful living! This kind of living would conform to the purpose for which human beings were created, redeemed, and called into fellowship with the Creator.

Wisdom is the ancient system of values handed down by God. It makes it possible for us to live by the sovereign Lord's divinely ordained principles, which prove to be in the best interests of both the individual and society. So let us look further into the Old Testament idea of wisdom.

There is no better place to start than the book of Proverbs. Most cultures include proverbs in their heritage. They are tested and true maxims preserved for the good and the education of succeeding generations. Usually they are pithy and pointed sayings designed to catch the attention and stick in the memory. All of us have catalogued in our minds such sayings as "A stitch in time saves nine," or "Forewarned is forearmed." Proverbs is similar, but it is also part of God's inspired word.

THE PURPOSE OF PROVERBS

The introduction to the book of Proverbs states its purpose clearly:

> *The proverbs of Solomon son of David, king of Israel:*
> *for attaining wisdom and discipline;*
> *for understanding words of insight;*
> *for acquiring a disciplined and prudent life,*
> *doing what is right and just and fair;*
> *for giving prudence to the simple,*
> *knowledge and discretion to the young—*
> *let the wise listen and add to their learning,*
> *and let the discerning get guidance—*
> *for understanding proverbs and parables,*
> *the sayings and riddles of the wise.*
> *The fear of the LORD is the beginning of knowledge,*
> *but fools despise wisdom and discipline.*
>
> PROVERBS 1:1-7

It is important to note that this introduction clearly states the practical usefulness of the Proverbs, in terms such as *wisdom, discipline, insight, prudence, knowledge, discretion,* and *guidance.*

Wisdom

Wisdom is not an abstract concept unrelated to life. On the contrary, wisdom enables one to avoid the distractions and wasted opportunities of an ill disciplined life. It provides insights into life's mysteries, banishes the mists of uncertainty and confusion, and substitutes the calm, measured decisions of prudence for the impulsive actions of ill-conceived recklessness. Wisdom imparts knowledge where wishful thinking once reigned supreme. It fosters the discretion of angels, who fear to tread where fools rush in heedless. It offers a sure and steady guide rather than a haphazard stumbling after the latest fad or foible.

Discipline

Wisdom requires discipline—instruction, training, correction, and the development of moral character. Proverbs is full of references to discipline. Consider the following:

> *My son, do not despise the LORD's discipline*
> *and do not resent his rebuke.*
>
> PROVERBS 3:11

Discipline will not always tell you what you want to hear but it will tell you what you need to know!

> *The evil deeds of a wicked man ensnare him;*
> *the cords of his sin hold him fast.*
> *He will die for lack of discipline,*
> *led astray by his own great folly.*
>
> PROVERBS 5:22-23

No one ever died from living a disciplined life, but many have died before they ever got around to developing one.

> *The corrections of discipline are the way to life.*
>
> PROVERBS 6:23

Any critic can tell you what you're doing wrong. But discipline will show you how to do it right.

> *Whoever loves discipline loves knowledge,*
> *but he who hates correction is stupid.*
>
> PROVERBS 12:1

Who is the stupid person? The one who learns from mistakes and makes corrections, or the one who goes on repeating them and simply makes a mess?

Discipline is vitally necessary for the development of a lifestyle that pleases God and brings blessing to others. The late Tom Landry, the legendary coach of the Dallas Cowboys and a committed believer, said, "The job of a coach is to make men do what they don't want to do, in order to be what they've always wanted to be." Some athletes think their natural talents are so great that they do not need to practice, stay in shape, or work out with the team. But if they want to be the superstars they think they are, they will have to do the things that they, in their own warped understanding, regard as unnecessary and unpleasant.

Tom Landry's comments apply to all who take seriously the business of being what they have "always wanted to be" and who seek to be "all God intended" them to be. Discipline is a major component of wisdom.

Understanding

Hebrew poetry uses parallelism, which means stating the same idea twice in different ways. This means that *wisdom* and *understanding* are used almost synonymously at times. Even so, *understanding* does have a special meaning. In 1 Kings 3:9, *understanding* describes Solomon's ability to distinguish between right and wrong. To gain understanding in this sense means to have the God-given capacity to "discern between" one thing and another. Understanding requires the ability to discriminate between options, using some objective standard of evaluation.

King Solomon once had to discern between the rival claims of two women to one baby (see 1 Kings 3:16-28). Only one of the women could be the mother, and only the mother had the right to claim the baby. Solomon announced that he should just divide the child in half with a sword so that each woman could have her share—knowing, of course, that the real mother would give her child up to the other woman rather than see it killed. By means of this risky challenge, Solomon identified the true mother, distinguished between the competing claims, discriminated the real from the fake mother, discerned the truth, and made his decision. That's understanding.

> *Discretion will protect you,*
> *and understanding will guard you.*
> PROVERBS 2:11

Failing to discriminate between the merits of two alternatives leaves one vulnerable to choosing unwisely the one that will be harmful.

> *Wisdom is supreme; therefore get wisdom.*
> *Though it cost all you have, get understanding.*
> PROVERBS 4:7

Understanding is infinitely precious, and without it we may lose everything.

> *A man of knowledge uses words with restraint,*
> *and a man of understanding is even-tempered.*
> PROVERBS 17:27

The person who can see only his own point of view may insist on it with such great vigor that he loses perspective, while the person who sees both sides of an issue and weighs them carefully is much more likely to respond with emotional equilibrium and considered judgment.

Prudence

The prudent life is described as "doing what is right and just and fair." The old-fashioned virtue of prudence has been defined as "the ability to make the right choice in specific situations." This understanding of prudence is very close to the classical virtues of justice and temperance. Justice is defined as "fairness, honesty, lawfulness, and the ability to keep one's promises," while temperance is "self-discipline, the control of unruly human passions and appetites."[21]

Doing what is right means adhering to correct standards. There is a clear example of this in what the children of Israel were told:

> Do not have two differing measures in your house—
> one large, one small. You must have accurate and
> honest weights and measures. DEUT. 25:14-15

The laws presented in Deuteronomy and other places in the Old Testament did not allow any changing of the weights. Measurements remained constant, no matter who was selling or who was buying.

I can still remember the feelings of apprehension I experienced as a boy when the Weights and Measures inspector periodically arrived, unannounced, at my father's store and checked the weights and measures to see if they were accurate according to government standards. My father did not share my apprehension because he was as honest as the day is long. Nevertheless, we were required to get the weights and measures right, and if through the process of normal wear and tear the weights had become inaccurate or the measures had been dented, replacements had to be procured. What is right, is right; what is fair, is fair; and these values do not change.

The attitude that says, "I can do whatever I like in the privacy of my own home, and it is irrelevant to my standing in public," did not wash in those days, and it should not in ours. What a man is in his house on his own is what he really is. One set of standards rules at home and in business.

Biblical prudence not only dictates that actions should be right but also that they should be just. While there is an obvious connection between the two, a just action requires that decisions relating to it be appropriate to the situation, as we convey when we say, "Let the punishment fit the crime."

Fairness
Every little child has concepts of fairness. Every parent at some time or other has been alarmed to hear bloodcurdling screams from one of their progeny only to discover, on arriving out of breath at the scene of the crime, that Junior is screaming blue murder because his sibling has gotten the last green candy that he wanted and "it's not fair!" For little people fair usually means, "I have lost the advantage that by right belongs to me!" This, of course, is not what Proverbs meant by fair, although youngsters certainly aren't the only ones who operate by this definition!

The real meaning of fairness is "behaving uprightly." *Upright* is a word that makes people nervous, maybe because it is too close to *uptight*. But there is no more connection between *upright* and *uptight* than between *meek* and *weak*. The upright are those who believe that what God says is right, seek to do what he says, and thus live rightly. Because we live in community rather than in isolation, this usually includes treating people rightly. To be fair, therefore, has vertical connections with the divine and horizontal connections with other people.

WHAT DOES IT MEAN TO BE FOOLISH?
What is your definition of a fool? Is it a stupid person? a class clown? someone who doesn't take life seriously? Let's take a look at a very serious definition. Blaise Pascal, the brilliant French mathematician and philosopher, wrote:

> There are only three kinds of persons: those who serve
> God having found him; others who are occupied in seek-
> ing him, not having found him; while the remainder
> live without seeking him and without having found
> him. The first are reasonable and happy, the last are
> foolish and unhappy; those between are unhappy and
> reasonable.[22]

By Pascal's definition, a foolish person is one who is living without seeking God and, consequently, not finding him. This is also the essence of foolishness in Proverbs.

There once was a woman who was married to a man who didn't deserve her. So what's new? But in this case he was extra bad, and she was quite extraordinarily special. He was a fool in the biblical sense of the word. That does not mean he was stupid, dumb, or given to zany humor. It means that he despised wisdom—he was opposed to all that we have been talking about, in a surly and mean-spirited way.

His name was Nabal, which, incidentally, means "fool" in the Hebrew. (His mother must have been no fool to recognize one so early!) He got himself into deep trouble with soon-to-be-king David, who was in no mood to be messed with. And if it had not been for Nabal's wife, Abigail, whom we are told was "intelligent and beautiful," he would have been summarily dealt with by His Irate Majesty and his men. As it happened, Abigail demonstrated wisdom, discipline, understanding, and prudence by intercepting the king, making amends, and averting disaster. When her husband found out how close to death he had been because of his own behavior, he promptly had a massive coronary and died anyway. David, meanwhile, comforted the grieving widow (who apparently wasn't too distraught that the old fool had passed on), married her, and she lived happily ever after (1 Samuel 25).

Great story? Yes. But more to the point: Great wisdom, great values, and great decisions added up to a great woman. And David was a lucky man to find such a treasure.

Now that we have explored some of the meanings of wisdom, and have seen how it relates to values and decision making, we need to press on to find out where this wisdom is to be found and how it can be nurtured and nourished in daily life.

THE BEGINNING OF WISDOM, THE BASIS OF VALUES

The fear of the LORD is a fountain of life,
turning a man from the snares of death.

PROVERBS 14:27

One of my numerous grandsons, Drew, went to his first baseball game when he was about two and a half years old. He sat with his father in the crowd at Wrigley Field in Chicago and watched the Chicago Cubs go through their annual disappearing act. But he enjoyed the experience and talked to me on the phone about it.

"What did you see, Drew?" I asked him.

"One, two, three, four, five, touchdown!" he replied with great enthusiasm.

I wasn't sure if he was confused about the game he had been watching, or if the reason for the Cubs' lack of success was that they were confused about which game they were playing! But my daughter came on the phone and clarified the situation. "He's confused, Dad. He saw the numbers on the scoreboard, and because he's learning his numbers, his alphabet, baseball, and football all at the same time, he's a little mixed up!"

Being an Englishman, I fully understand the necessity of learning my alphabet and numbers—if not baseball and American football—because all of us, however accomplished, must begin with basics. Shakespeare began with his alphabet, Einstein with his numbers.

One, two, three, four, five, with or without a touchdown.

A, B, C, D, E, F, with or without a home run.

In all walks of life we must start at the beginning and begin with the basics. So let's talk about the basics of values, the foundations of wisdom. The 123s and the ABCs.

THE FEAR OF THE LORD

The introduction to Proverbs ends with 1:7:

> *The fear of the LORD is the beginning of knowledge,*
> *but fools despise wisdom and discipline.*

The same thought is expressed slightly differently in Proverbs 9:10:

> *The fear of the LORD is the beginning of wisdom,*
> *and knowledge of the Holy One is understanding.*

Although, as we have seen, *knowledge, discipline,* and *understanding* have different connotations, they are often used interchangeably. But in these and many other powerful statements in Proverbs it is the "fear of the Lord" that is the basis, the foundation, the starting point of wisdom or a system of values from which our decisions originate.

Now, if the fear of the Lord is so important, we need to know what it means. Recently when I quoted a verse that included the phrase "the fear of the Lord," someone came to me after the talk and said, "I was brought up in a religious system where we were basically trained to be scared of God. I spent all my years as a kid feeling guilty because I'd been doing stuff I shouldn't have done, waiting for the heavens to drop in on my head and for God to zap me. In the end I just threw it all over. I figured if he was going to get me, he would get me, and there was nothing I could do about it. So for twenty-five years I just did what I wanted and figured when God was good and ready he'd get me. But then one day I found your church, where you weren't into that kind of stuff, and I discovered God loved me unconditionally. Everything changed. I knew I was loved. Forgiven. It was so free, so friendly and fun, and now you're trying to put 'the fear of God' into us again! I don't need this stuff. I'm out of here!'"

WHAT THE FEAR OF THE LORD IS NOT

This is a fairly common experience, and we should begin by explaining what the fear of the Lord is not. If God were mean and vindictive and unforgiving, if he acted arbitrarily and inconsistently, if he judged with partiality and punished unjustly, then we would be right to fear him in the way we would fear an abusive parent or an oppressive government. We would avoid him at all costs. We would cower in a corner, freeze at the thought of his presence, resent every overture by his Spirit, react to every intimation of grace, run from any commitment to his cause, respond to every promise with dismissive skepticism, and miss no opportunity to convince ourselves of the wrongness of his attitude toward us and the rectitude of our attitude toward him.

But the fact is, Scripture emphasizes the lovingkindness and mercy of God through both testaments. In dealing with his chosen people Israel, God demonstrated remarkable forbearance and patience. He showed himself repeatedly to be the God who gives a second chance—and a third and a fourth and a ninety-ninth! When he entered our world in the person of Jesus Christ, we were treated to a portrait of God in a human being. This portrait left no room for confusion as to the true character of the invisible God. Jesus demonstrated God's attitude toward us as he reached out to care, to heal, to forgive us, and answer our questions. He proved to us that God is approachable, that He understands our frailty, that the Holy God actually wants to be in relationship with us.

However, any relationship requires that each party recognize the true identity of the other party. The "fear of the Lord" then, is an attitude toward God that rightly recognizes and relates to who he is. And we can only rightly relate to who God is if we *understand* who he is. Being scared of and repelled by God is not a helpful reaction.

So what does it mean to "fear the Lord?" My good friend Phil Hacking, an Anglican minister, and his wife were hiking in the English countryside. They came to a place where a farmer had built a fence across the public pathway. Phil's wife said to him, "There's the farmer up on the hill—let's go and tell him that he has no right putting a fence across a public path." So they climbed the hill to where the farmer and his employee were working, and they confronted him. He stopped his work and listened politely to their indignant expostulations. While Phil was expressing his righteous indignation, however, he was puzzled to see that his wife, who had insisted he should complain, was making faces at him behind the farmer's back, telling him to stop. He ignored her, however, and said his piece. The farmer promised to rectify the error, and they went on their way.

"Didn't you recognize him?" asked his wife.

"No," replied Phil, "he was just the farmer, and he needed to be told."

"You idiot!" she replied. "That was Prince Charles. The Prince of Wales!"

"Well," said Phil, surprised and abashed but undaunted, "it doesn't matter who he is. He shouldn't have built the fence where he did."

"I agree," she answered, "but you could have shown a little more respect!"

"You're right," Phil admitted. "If I'd known who he was, I'd have shown a little more respect."

If we knew who God really is, we'd show him "a little more respect." The problem in the modern world is that too often there is an inadequate knowledge of God. There's a lot of speculation as to who God is and what he's like. But we need to operate on the basis of revelation, not speculation. It is one thing for us to express what we *think*

God is like; it is an entirely different thing for us to recognize what God *says* he is like. Speculation at the expense of revelation leads only to mystification.

What better place to discover who God is than in his self-description? When talking to Moses on Mount Sinai, God described himself as: "The compassionate and gracious God, slow to anger, abounding in love and faithfulness, maintaining love to thousands, and forgiving wickedness, rebellion, and sin" (Exod. 34:6-7).

Isn't that wonderful? Isn't it exciting to know that God is compassionate and gracious and forgiving and slow to anger and faithful and loving and kind? But that's only part of the picture. For he went on to say, "Yet he does not leave the guilty unpunished; he punishes the children and their children for the sin of the fathers to the third and fourth generation" (Exod. 34:7).

We must make sure that we have a well-rounded picture of who God is. God is fundamentally holy, good, just, right, and fair. If we contravene his laws, if we insult who he is, resist his guidance, and ignore his direction, then he must respond in a manner that is in keeping with his holy, just, right, and fair character. He must, if he is true to himself, deal with us in righteous judgment. Truly it is "a terrible thing to fall into the hands of the living God" (Heb. 10:31, NLT).

But if we will admit that we were wrong and repent of what we have done, he will overwhelm us with his grace, loving kindness, and forgiveness.

In fact, God's love and grace is directly related to his righteousness and holiness. And our appreciation of his forgiveness is in direct proportion to our knowledge of his judgment.

All this comes together in the Cross of our Lord Jesus, which shows God's intense disgust for our rebellion and sin and demonstrates his intense desire to forgive us. Do you want a vision of divine wrath, intense holiness, and righteous judgment? Look at the Cross.

Do you want to know divine love, mercy, and grace? Look at the Cross! Don't look at either dimension of God's character in isolation. Don't try to grasp grace without seeing judgment. Don't expect to appreciate God's mercy without being stunned by his holiness.

WHAT THE FEAR OF THE LORD IS

I suggest that the fear of the Lord is an attitude toward God that shrinks back in fear before experiencing forgiveness, and draws close in awe when forgiven. The unforgiven sinner, overwhelmed with feelings of shame before a holy God, rightly draws back in fear until she hears the invitation to draw near, which she does with a compelling sense of awe. There is no contradiction here. Alpine climbers revel in the thrill of scaling the majestic heights but must never lose sight of the fearful awesomeness of the mountain. Deep-sea fishermen toil with joy and garner a harvest in the foaming waves, but they know they must never treat the mighty, rolling ocean with anything but respect. Small aircraft pilots, they tell me, come in two varieties: old ones and bold ones. There are no old, bold ones! Or to quote the pilots' proverb, "All take-offs are optional, but all landings are required!" Those who enjoy the freedom of flying like a bird do so conscious of the terrific awesomeness of the heavens in which they soar and the terrible hardness of the earth over which they do it.

The fear of the Lord involves glad submission to his gracious majesty. When we "fear the Lord," our overriding desire is to honor his majesty and respect his authority while appropriating his grace, reveling in his love, basking in his forgiveness, and seeking only to please him. And our deepest concern is that we do not besmirch his glory or dishonor his name. This is what it means to fear the Lord; this understanding is fundamental to our system of values and the decisions we make that shape our lives.

Some people may be concerned that I am majoring on Old Testament concepts that are no longer relevant in these days of grace. Is it so important to think about the fear of the Lord anymore? Didn't Jesus describe God as a loving Father, and doesn't the first letter of John tell us that perfect love casts out fear? Aren't we finished with this God of judgment? Not if we note the New Testament's references to this healthy, holy fear. For example, one of the main criticisms that God levels at the human race is, "there is no fear of God before their eyes" (Rom. 3:18).

Moreover, one of the greatest motivational statements of the New Testament is, "Let us purify ourselves from everything that contaminates body and spirit, perfecting holiness out of reverence for God [fear of the Lord]" (2 Cor. 7:1).

It is worth noting the description of the early church given in Acts 9. This was a church that had greatly feared the persecution of Saul of Tarsus. After Saul was converted the church entered a time of peace and thanksgiving. The Scriptures say in verse 31 that they were strengthened, they were encouraged in the Spirit, and they grew numerically. But all this happened as they were "living in the fear of the Lord." They were evangelistic. They were worshipful. They had tremendous fellowship. They had a great time together. And they were multiplying dramatically. It was apparently what some people today would call "a fun church to be part of." But fun or not, this remarkable church operated under the umbrella of acknowledging the Lord, being conscious of his awesome majesty, and the necessity for their glad submission to him. They lived in the fear of the Lord.

So let's accept the legitimacy of developing a keen fear of the Lord today also, without in any sense losing sight of the wonders of grace and the thrills of forgiveness and fellowship with him. And let's look further into how we can develop this attitude in ourselves.

HOW DO WE COME TO A FEAR OF THE LORD?

Wisdom does not grow on trees; neither does the fear of the Lord just happen. There are steps to be taken, as outlined in Proverbs.

My son, if you accept my words
and store up my commands within you,
turning your ear to wisdom
and applying your heart to understanding,
and if you call out for insight
and cry aloud for understanding,
and if you look for it as for silver
and search for it as for hidden treasure,
then you will understand the fear of the LORD,
and find the knowledge of God.

PROVERBS 2:1-5

Wisdom is the result not only of desire but of active seeking. If we acknowledge that fools despise wisdom, we also acknowledge that all of us have to come to the point of deciding whether or not we want to be bothered with what God says. There's a Nabal in all of us. There's a heart that is resistant and a will that is rebellious.

Sometimes it takes a mammoth step for us to start looking at things God's way after a lifetime of doing it our own way. For many people it takes a monumental crisis for them to begin to look at where society's values have taken them and likewise to take a hard look at what God has said. A friend of mine who had lived a number of years in a rebellious, independently-minded attitude said that it was only when he "became sick and tired of being sick and tired" that he returned to the principles he had learned in his childhood and rejected in his adolescence.

There is no shortage of discouraged, disillusioned people who have felt let down by their lives. Marvin Hamlisch was the toast of Los Angeles the night in April 1974 when he won three Oscars at the Academy Awards. But he said, "Three Oscars in my hands, and I come home and empty the cat litter. I had thought that success would make me happy but it didn't."[23]

Anthony Quinn, the Oscar-winning actor, star of more than one hundred movies, shortly before he died at the age of eighty-six reportedly said, "I'm like a guy playing a horn. There's a note I hear inside me but I can't play it yet. Someday I'm going to hit that note." Whether or not he ever defined that note or was able to hit it before he died we have no way of knowing. We do know he lived life to the full by Hollywood's standards. He married three times, had at least three mistresses who together bore him nine sons and four daughters, and enjoyed "the best of everything." But he still spoke openly as if he had missed out on discovering that elusive "note" sounding in the depth of his soul.

We don't have to look far to find illustrations of lives filled with the emptiness of self-gratification. Not a few people from all walks of life arrive at this point of dismay and finally, almost as a last resort, begin to consider God. But at least they begin to explore his truth. They are open to mining for wisdom.

But not everybody who begins to question their value system and its failure to come through for them is willing to explore the truth of God with the tenacity and expectancy of a gold miner. While they are unhappy with the way things are, they suspect that they might be unhappier if they made changes in God's direction. To surrender the "self" as the primary value and to adopt God's way means giving up the autonomy that, although it has failed to satisfy, is still cherished as possibly a person's greatest treasure. Furthermore, rejecting society's version of what is "normal" would open a person to charges by friends and relatives of "not living in the real world."

Then there are those who are interested in a quick-fix religious experience without necessarily being willing to turn their ear to wisdom and applying their heart to understanding. In such cases the quick fix is certainly quick but "fixes" nothing.

HOW DOES A FEAR OF THE LORD AFFECT MY BEHAVIOR?
Practically speaking, how do we behave if our lives are governed by decisions based on the fear of the Lord?

Hate Evil

To fear the LORD is to hate evil.

PROVERBS 8:13

I believe everybody on God's green earth finds something utterly distasteful and despicable—something they classify as evil. I don't believe there is anyone so totally reprobate that they cannot condemn at least one thing as out-and-out evil. Oskar Schindler, whose story was immortalized in Steven Spielberg's movie *Schindler's List,* was a renowned drunkard and womanizer who treated his wife, Emilie, dreadfully but risked his life and lost his fortune countering the evil he saw in the Nazis. He was no paragon of virtue, but he believed in evil and he knew it when he saw it! Everybody recognizes evil in some form and hates it. But the trouble is that everybody has their own special hatred for a specific kind of evil while simultaneously cherishing a secret love for another evil. To hate evil does not mean to hate it selectively but to be willing to see evil in all its manifestations from the divine perspective. This will mean recognizing as evil some things that I now cherish, becoming indignant about some things that I now casually tolerate but that God abhors.

Years ago, in our youth work in England, we had a young boy called Kenny whose main gift appeared to be breaking windows. Nothing we said or did managed to persuade him that there was something fundamentally wrong about his approach to glass in frames. Until we put him in charge of the windows. Then his perspective changed by 180 degrees. He saw things through the eyes of leadership, and his behavior was transformed. He was on the inside looking out instead of being on the outside breaking in. And with the change of heart came a dramatic alteration in his value system! He became a lover of windows and a hater of destructive tendencies. And (not surprisingly) he decided to break no more and (more surprisingly) to deal severely with those who did. A change of perspective will do that!

But there's another problem we all face when it comes to confronting evil. Have you ever been enjoying a meal in front of the television when suddenly you discovered you were viewing pictures of a famine? Did you lose your appetite or change the channel? Do you ever watch movies that portray the most incredible violence and thoroughly enjoy it because the bad guys "got theirs"? And have you ever been unmoved when you saw news pictures of real people being blown away? You know what was happening, don't you? You were being desensitized by familiarity with evil. The fact that around the world people were actually being blown away was no longer a concern.

It is possible for us to be desensitized to things simply because we've become used to them, and we are often unable or unwilling to evaluate what is happening to us. We get so used to people calling wrong right and evil good that we lose track of our bearings. We may find ourselves doing evil without knowing it or, worse, without even worrying about it.

But there's one safety net. The fear of the Lord will sensitize us to evil. When we read regularly in God's Word about the activities and attitudes God hates, we won't take them for granted so easily in our daily lives. Read what Jesus said about hypocrisy; read what the prophet Amos said about injustice and oppression of the poor; read what Paul said about the devastating effects of sexual immorality. All of these are serious issues to a holy God, who explains his displeasure with them very specifically. As we adopt God's view and God's values, our hearts and minds will begin to experience pain and horror when we see or hear evil. We will begin to hate what the Lord hates, and this will help us keep our values in place, our decisions in line, and our lives on track.

Fear the Right Thing

He who fears the LORD has a secure fortress.
PROVERBS 14:26

Franklin D. Roosevelt once told the people of the United States, "We have nothing to fear but fear itself." That was great presidential rhetoric and was possibly a very helpful thing to say to a discouraged nation, but it was incorrect. To tell people that there's nothing to fear but fear itself is to ignore the one fear that is necessary: the fear of the Lord. When "the fear of the Lord" is in place, then we can say with assurance, "Fear the Lord and you have nothing else to fear." Why? Because the fear of the Lord is a secure fortress. "We have nothing to fear but the Lord himself."

Rupert Brooks was a poet who knew firsthand the ghastly, inhumane conditions of the trenches in the First World War, in which he eventually met an untimely death. He wrote a poem called "Safety" which included the following lines:

Safe shall be my going.
Secretly armed against all death's endeavour;
Safe though all safety's lost; safe where men fall;
And if these poor limbs die, safest of all.

In the midst of the fearful conditions of the WWI trenches, Brooks had found a secure fortress in the Lord. And he could say bravely that he was "safe though all safety's lost."

Far from the battlefields of twentieth-century Europe, people still struggle with fears that could easily be assuaged by discovering the "fear of the Lord." Men sometimes experience feelings of insecurity which lead to all kinds of behavioral excesses and relational problems. I have met a number of men who are totally threatened by being married to sharp women who earn more than they do. They fear that their masculinity is in question, that they are failing to meet the standard of the successful and competent man. Their inability to cope produces deep anger that at times bursts in verbal and even physical abuse. These men, impoverished in their own manhood through their lack of security as persons, take the only course in which they feel superior—physical domination of women.

The fear of the Lord would go a long way in dealing with such unacceptable behavior. First of all, if a man would recognize that he will answer to an awesome Lord for his abusive treatment of God's creation, he would act differently. And second, in reverencing the Lord, a man would discover that the Lord made him uniquely special in his own right. He would realize that he has no need to compete where he cannot and no cause to worry if he comes out on the short end of the comparison. The "fear of the Lord" would truly become his "secure fortress" and his savvy wife would be eternally grateful.

Look for Safety

I was thinking recently that the old-fashioned, rigid rules of my fundamentalist heritage, which I was less than enthusiastic about as I grew up, nevertheless delivered me from a lot of things that could be called, at the risk of seeming overly dramatic, "the snares of death." The three golden rules were No Smoking, No Drinking, and No Sex before Marriage. As I embarked on my business career and later served in the Royal Marines, I quickly discovered that I was in a tiny minority as far as these rules were concerned. I spent a lot of time living in close quarters with people who not only regarded my behavior as odd but openly questioned whether I didn't have some problems that they thought were their duty to solve! But now years later, I sometimes wonder what happened to all my smoking, drinking, carousing companions.

Smoking. I now note that smoking is injurious to my health. The Surgeon General says so on every packet of cigarettes. In fact, the American Medical Association reports, "Cigarette smoking causes more premature deaths each year than . . . AIDS, fire, cocaine, car accidents, heroin, homicide, alcohol, [and] suicide . . . put together."[24] I'm glad I never started! And I'm glad I didn't listen to my friends.

Drinking. In regard to drinking—which, in the circles I was required to move, was considered a rite of passage, a badge of manhood—I now hear athletes and actors, businessmen and wives of presidents, the rich and famous, and the poor and unknown be-moaning their alcohol-induced fate and seeking help. One celebrity openly admitted that under the influence he'd "go from jocose to amorous and then to bellicose and then lachrymose and finally co-matose." The state of Wisconsin, where my family and I have made our home and established the center of our ministry for more than thirty years, has an unenviable record when it comes to alcohol. The U.S. Center for Disease Control reported in 1987 that in Wisconsin alcohol was the fourth leading cause of death after heart disease, cancer, and stroke. It was also reported that alcohol was a major fac-tor in no fewer than 258 traffic deaths and that we led the nation in binge drinking, chronic drinking, and driving under the influence. The CDC also reported that even though the official drinking age was twenty-one, no less than 81 percent of young people between the ages of twelve and seventeen had consumed alcohol. I'm glad I never started that either!

Carousing. Then there's the issue of sex before and outside of mar-riage. One of today's biggest issues is "safe sex." The reason for this is the prevalence of what we politely call STDs—sexually transmitted diseases. If you have sex with someone, you might catch what they've got, who caught it from someone else, who got it from someone else! I spoke recently with a missionary doctor who has devoted his life to caring for the poor people of Sao Paulo, Brazil. He told me that he regularly spends approximately one hour with each patient, dealing not only with their medical symptoms but with the underlying causes of their maladies. But when he deals with STDs he traces meticu-lously all the sexual partners from whom and to whom the diseases have passed. No wonder people are running scared and going in for "safe sex," as if there were such a thing. Well, actually there is! It's the old-fashioned approach that the Bible teaches and my fundamentalist heritage taught: No sex outside of marriage.

CONCLUSION

Truly the fear of the Lord is a fountain of life that turns us from the snares of death; it is a secure fortress; and it teaches us to hate evil. And it is the beginning of wisdom—the fundamental basis of a system of values, and a repository of solid data from which sound decisions are made.

"The fear of the Lord" is all about developing an appropriate attitude towards God. It means that we know him as he is rather than as the person we hope he is. It means respecting him as we ought rather than treating him as we shouldn't.

There are great advantages to rightly relating to the Lord—we will be protected from that which harms and introduced to that which enriches. Decisions that are based on a desire to honor the Lord and not to displease him are smart, beneficial, life affirming, and right!

Marriage is an institution in whose maintenance and purity the
public is deeply interested, for it is the foundation of the family
and society without which there would be neither civilization nor progress.

THE UNITED STATES SUPREME COURT

*A*bout fifty years after the American Republic was founded,
French philosopher and sociologist Alexis de Tocqueville
came to see firsthand the remarkable sociological experiment called
the United States of America. Then he went home and wrote a book
called *Democracy in America,* which as far as I can tell is more often
quoted than read. Be that as it may, along with many other insightful
observations he said:

> Certainly of all countries in the world, America is the
> one in which the marriage tie is most respected and
> wherethe highest and truest conception of conjugal
> happiness has been conceived.[25]

High praise indeed! In light of what de Tocqueville had to say about
the early days of the American Republic, and what the Supreme
Court stated about the importance of marriage, we need to ask,
"What happened?"

America now leads the Western democracies in divorce. At least 50 percent of new marriages end in divorce. The National Association of Evangelicals reported in the 1990s that, in the 30-plus years since 1960, teen sexual activity had doubled, cohabitation had increased by 600 percent, illegitimate births had increased by more than 500 percent, teen suicides had tripled, and the American Psychological Association had rated "decline of the nuclear family as the number one threat to mental health."

Would de Tocqueville recognize America if he returned today? How could social mores change so drastically?

SOCIAL VALUES LEAD TO SOCIAL CONDITION

I believe these social changes are due to changes in our values as a society, and I am not alone in this opinion. While the America that de Tocqueville visited could not accurately be described as a Christian nation, biblical values were in fact widely respected. But that is no longer the case. Secularization has taken over, and this is particularly true in attitudes toward marriage and family. But what does that mean? Carl F. H. Henry has written:

> Instead of recognizing Yahweh as the source and stipulator of truth and the good, contemporary thought reduces all reality to impersonal processes and events, and insists that man, himself, creatively imposes upon the Cosmos and upon history the only values that they will ever bear. This dethronement of God and enthronement of man as lord of the universe, this eclipse of the supernatural and exaggeration of the natural, has precipitated an intellectual and moral crisis that escorts Western civilization, despite its brilliant technological achievements, ever nearer to anguished collapse and atheistic suffocation.[26]

Secularization is what happens when humans refuse to fear the Lord or recognize Yahweh as the source and stipulator of truth. They then creatively impose their own values on their world, working from their own individualized set of assumptions.

There's nothing wrong with working from assumptions unless, of course, the assumptions are wrong. And on the subject of marriage and family, secular thought holds some basic assumptions that are seriously questionable. Two of the major ones are that (1) marriage was a human idea—something that human beings dreamed up as they developed in their relational skills and addressed the problems of living in society; and that (2) societies go through an evolutionary process of development.

This line of reasoning leads to the conclusion that in America's early days, the old approach to marriage and family was perfectly appropriate, but in the modern era it has been superseded by "alternative lifestyles," which in secular thought are not only perfectly legitimate but are probably an improvement on what used to be.

Maris Vinovskis, a professor at the University of Michigan, was quoted by *Time* magazine in a special Fall 1992 issue as saying, "The fact of change is the one constant throughout the history of the family. The family is the most flexible adaptive institution. It is constantly evolving."[27]

Once it is assumed that marriage and the family are purely human ideas, there will be no restraints on human attempts to improve these societal structures. Andrea Engber is convinced that she has come up with a better alternative than marriage. She is a single mother who admitted that she was "living with a guy that I didn't want to marry" and said, "I stayed with him because I wanted a child. But I didn't want him." After the child was born, she lost her job, so she started a magazine called SingleMOTHER in order that "women in my position could support each other." She added, "I wouldn't change anything I've done. You only have to look at the divorce rate to see that marriage isn't working." Her reason for an alternative? Marriage isn't working. Her solution? Single parenthood.

But saying that marriage isn't working is benign stuff compared to much of the rhetoric that many influential people are leveling at this ancient institution. *U.S. News & World Report* documented instances of female victimization from around the world.[28] The article noted that "the 1993 U.N. Human Development Report found that there still is no country that treats its women as well as its men." One doesn't have to be a radical feminist to know that there is a lot of truth to that statement.

I have been a pastor long enough to know that there are many marriages that look perfectly normal on the outside but are actually desperately dysfunctional. Many a smiling face hides a breaking heart; and many a designer jacket, a broken rib. Terrorism in the home is a highly emotive phrase, but it may be an apt description of the things that are being done by some people to their marriage partners.

So two of the main reasons we are given for the desire to bring about changes in the institutions of marriage and family are that it isn't working and that marriage in some way lends itself to the violation of women, and occasionally men. Therefore, on both counts, people say, "Marriage is broken—let's find an alternative. Marriage and family have always changed, so let's bring about some more changes."

CHANGING DEFINITIONS OF MARRIAGE AND FAMILY
We can certainly acknowledge that the family has seen dramatic changes during the course of human history. In the beginning there was a family—Adam and Eve and their boys—which, in modern parlance, was extremely dysfunctional! As time went on, the emphasis was placed on clans and tribes, then extended families. Only since the Industrial Revolution have we become familiar with the "nuclear family"—the *Ozzie and Harriet* model. So it would be foolish to deny

that family structures have changed over the years for various socio-logical, economic, and geographical reasons.

In the same way, it is clear that attitudes toward marriage have changed. In biblical history we can see that monogamy came first, then polygamy, and then concubines. And with these changes came all kinds of problems. So we can agree that there have been changes in the structures of marriage and family down through the centuries. But not that all of these changes have been beneficial!

We need not subscribe to the theory that marriage is a human idea and that it is evolving in increasingly better forms. That, of course, is exactly what secularists are saying and what they want us to believe. Maris Vinovskis stated this point of view breathlessly:

> It is reasonable to ask whether in the future there will be a family at all. Given the propensity for divorce, the growing number of adults who choose to remain single, the declining popularity of having children, and the evaporation of the time families spend together, another way may eventually evolve. In any event, as the nuclear family dissolves what is likely to evolve is a sort of make your own family approach . . . the family of choice.[29]

Not everybody is as prepared to write off marriage and the family as *Time,* even though people are eagerly looking for ways to fix what they perceive to be the problems in the old institutions. Some of them have adopted the much subtler but no less challenging approach of simply redefining the institutions. So instead of the traditional definition of a family, which is "two or more persons related by birth, marriage, or adoption and residing together," they are advocating defining the family as "a group of people who love and care for each other."

Notice the emphasis on love and care. Who could quarrel with that? But why the refusal to incorporate commitment? The reasoning behind this is very easy to see. In previous generations there was a solid commitment to marriage, but often it was a commitment seriously lacking in love and caring intimacy. There was often bitterness and much suppressed anger and icy isolation within "committed" marriages. Many younger people who observed this in their parents' marriages have said, "No way am I going to get myself into a situation like that. If that's what the institution of marriage does for you, who needs it? What we need is warmth. What we need is intimacy. And if we can't find warmth and intimacy inside these cold, bitter, icy institutions, then we'll think of something better." We can readily sympathize with these concerns. But we have to question their naïve assumption that getting rid of commitment will in some way cause people to be more warm and intimate.

Take, for instance, the case of the young actress, Anne Heche. She had a two-year "relationship" with the famous actor-comedian Steve Martin, after which she entered into a highly publicized lesbian relationship with fellow actress Ellen DeGeneres. The glowing publicity in which this relationship was bathed led us to believe that we were witnessing two young women who had found in each other a loving, caring, nurturing experience, which, if not superior to what they could find in a traditional marriage, was certainly equal to it and should accordingly be universally accepted as equally valid.

Quite soon, the relationship ended in acrimony, and less than nine months later Anne Heche announced her engagement to Coleman Laffoon, a cameraman whom she had met in the course of her work.

There can be little doubt that Ms. Heche is looking for a relationship that will meet her deepest longings, and it would be reasonable to assume from her past experience that she is open to exploring numerous "options." But her recent history leads one to believe that the alternatives that she is exploring have done nothing to satisfy, and there is nothing in her lifestyle to suggest that she has discovered something that is superior to that which God clearly ordained from the beginning of creation—loving, caring, monogamous, heterosexual marriage.

We share the genuine concern of those who have been damaged by the institution of marriage. But we are also left with the uneasy feeling that there are underlying motives for rejecting marriage—motives that are not always voiced.

We still must wonder what kind of glorious confusion would reign if, in the midst of our personal confusion and the variety of our sources and opinions, we sought to "fix what's broke" in marriage by simply redefining it. For instance, try to understand what Garth Brooks said in response to a question about his apparent affirmation of same-sex marriages in his song, "We Shall Be Free." Brooks "clarified" his position by stating, "It's tough for me because I love the Bible. For those people that feel religiously that homosexuality is wrong, are they not as right as the people who feel homosexuality is right?"[30] How's that for confusion?

WHERE DOES THIS LEAVE US?
While there have been historical changes in human approaches to marriage and family, these changes have not led to an evolution of something superior to what was known before. It is a serious error to assume that marriage and family are simply human inventions that can be changed by human beings without any repercussions to our individual and community lives. There are serious problems in marriages and families—granted. But to discredit the institutions because of the problems is similar to the attempt of some British intellectuals to discredit the church because of World War I—a position that led G. K. Chesterton to comment, "They might as well say that the Ark was discredited by the Flood. . . . When the world goes wrong, it proves rather that the church is right. The church is justified, not because her children do not sin, but because they do."[31] In the same way, the institutions of marriage and family, far from being discred-

ited by their sinful abuse, are proven to be the right way to go. Marriages following divine principles have proved to be the greatest antidote to man's innate proclivity to abusive behavior in relationships.

TRIED AND TRUE STATEMENTS ABOUT MARRIAGE

There is nothing new about marriage being under attack. The Proverbs give powerful teaching on the subject of defending against the forces that would seek to undo the marital bond.

> *Wisdom will save you from the ways of wicked men,*
> *from men whose words are perverse,*
> *who leave the straight paths*
> *to walk in dark ways. . . .*
> *It will save you also from the adulteress,*
> *from the wayward wife with her seductive words,*
> *who has left the partner of her youth*
> *and ignored the covenant she made before God.*
> PROVERBS 2:12-13, 16-17

God Views Marriage as a Sacred Covenant

The word *covenant* is not used much today, so we need to be clear on its meaning. The unique relationship that existed between Israel and Jehovah was based on a covenant that Jehovah had initiated with Abram, a.k.a. Abraham. Called by the Lord to leave the relative comfort of his home in Ur of the Chaldees, Abram went! He went with nothing more to go on than a promise that he would be shown where to go and that he would be blessed when he got there. His destination was a land inhabited by people who were intent on staying there. Nevertheless, Jehovah made a covenant with Abram that stipulated, "To your descendants I give this land" (Genesis 15:18). Later on, when Abram was ninety-nine years old, Jehovah confirmed the covenant, saying,

> "I will establish my covenant as an everlasting covenant
> between me and you and your descendants after you for
> the generations to come, to be your God and the God
> of your descendants after you. The whole land of
> Canaan, where you are now an alien, I will give as an
> everlasting possession to you and your descendants after
> you; and I will be their God."
>
> Then God said to Abraham, "As for you, you must
> keep my covenant, you and your descendants after you
> for the generations to come." GENESIS 17:7-9

The covenant was as ingrained in the Israelite psyche as the Constitution is ingrained in the American psyche. Without the covenant there
would have been no Israel, just as without the Constitution there
would be no United States. Every Israelite knew that the nation operated under the covenant; every young Israelite was raised from his
earliest years with that understanding. All that they were and all that
they had and all that they ever hoped to be was wrapped up in the
covenant. Jehovah had chosen them to be his people for his own reasons and purposes; he had staked his reputation on being their God
and delivering on his promises; and all he asked of them was that they
respond by being his people and living according to his commands.
No Israelite would misunderstand the meaning of covenant.

Every part of Israelite life was covenant structured, and on that basis they entered into another covenant, the covenant of marriage.
They understood that marriage was God's idea, not man's. They recognized that it was to be lived out God's way, not theirs. They knew
that covenants involved promises and commitments, which they
made in a covenant to each other. Their own marriages were based on
the ancient statement God had made right at the beginning of human
history: "For this reason a man will leave his father and mother and be
united to his wife, and they will become one flesh" (Gen. 2:24).

The Israelites were far from perfect, which meant they had

less-than-perfect marriages. So Jehovah sent his prophets at regular intervals to remind them about the covenant he had made with them and the covenants they had made with each other before him. For example, when the people complained that their worship of the Lord was becoming meaningless, Malachi told them:

> You weep and wail because [God] no longer pays attention to your offerings or accepts them with pleasure from your hands. You ask, "Why?" It is because the LORD is acting as the witness between you and the wife of your youth, because you have broken faith with her, though she is your partner, the wife of your marriage covenant. Has not the LORD made them one? In flesh and spirit they are his. And why one? Because he was seeking godly offspring. So guard yourself in your spirit, and do not break faith with the wife of your youth.
>
> MALACHI 2:13-15

One + One = One

When two people are married in church by a minister, they are tacitly saying, "We want to be married in church by a minister because we recognize the divine dimension of marriage. We are making a covenant before God. We've got our witnesses who'll sign the marriage contract. Our friends and relatives are here to witness our covenant promises. But more important, God is our witness. We are making this solemn covenant commitment to each other before the Lord."

When we make a covenant before God, something marvelous is done by God. He takes two very different people, and in some remarkable way he makes them one. Remember Malachi's words: "Has not [the LORD] made them one? In flesh and spirit they are his" (2:15). To make two people one "in spirit" is different from making them one "in flesh." Put in very simple terms, when two people become one "in flesh," it means they have sexual intercourse. One of the ways in which this oneness is demonstrated is in the oneness of sexual enjoyment of each other.

But when two people are one "in spirit," it means something far beyond having sex. It means caring for a person rather than just enjoying a body, relating to someone of intrinsic worth whose fears and aspirations, whose loves and dislikes, whose beliefs and principles become part of your life. It means God is binding two lives together so that over the years, as they pass through changing circumstances, they will discover a oneness of spirit that enables them to respond in ways that serve only to deepen their love and commitment to each other. They become more and more deeply integrated into each other's personalities. They begin to see things through each other's eyes. They instinctively think each other's thoughts. My wife even finishes my sentences for me—not always the way I intended, but sometimes better than I could have done!

These two forms of oneness are related; they must not be separated from each other. It is therefore utterly wrong to be joined sexually with someone to whom one has not been joined spiritually.

The marriage covenant is a commitment we make before God, which introduces us to something that is done to us by God. But we may ask with Malachi, "Why one?" or Why does God do this? Why is he so concerned about male/female relationships that he should outline principles of behavior for them and even be involved in making them unique? The prophet's answer is what we need to hear: "Because he was seeking godly offspring" (2:15). All things being equal, when God joins two people together in spirit and they come together in flesh, there will be offspring. The coming together of spirit and flesh through divine covenant generally results in offspring, whom the parents have the responsibility to bring up in the fear and admonition of the Lord. This is what true wisdom teaches. These are the core values—the basis of family values.

The ancient Israelites, like modern people of industrialized Western democracies, had strayed far from these principles. Malachi needed to remind the Israelites that, even though in Moses' day the Lord had reluctantly allowed divorce in limited circumstances because of the hardness of the people's hearts, God's position was, "I hate divorce . . . and I hate a man's covering himself [or 'his wife,' NIV margin] with violence as well as with his garment" (Mal. 2:16). The Lord not only hates to see people breaking a covenant they made before him, but he also hates the kind of violent behavior that leads to this kind of breakdown. It is not only divorce that is the problem, but it is also the godless, ill-disciplined behavior that violates the spouse and leads to the breakdown of trust, care, and mutual concern, which so often ends in divorce.

My daughter, Judy Golz, in a doctoral dissertation submitted to New York University, came up with ample empirical evidence that the damage done to young people in intact but abusive families is not measurably different from that done to young people through the tragedy of divorce. It is not just divorce that God hates—it is the kind of behavior that so often leads to divorce.

Marriage as Companionship

This Malachi passage says that the man has left his partner in the marriage covenant. The word translated *partner* occurs on numerous occasions throughout Proverbs, often translated *friend*. So for example, Proverbs 17:17 states, "A friend loves at all times," and Proverbs 18:24, "There is a friend who sticks closer than a brother." Marriage is intended to be a companionship of two people who stick closer than anybody else to each other—who genuinely love at all times. It is a companionship of mutual caring.

Proverbs 27:6 gives us another clue about this kind of friendship: "Wounds from a friend can be trusted." Proverbs 27:9 adds, "The pleasantness of one's friend springs from his earnest counsel." Marriage is a relationship in which two friends come together, care for each other, confront each other to build each other up, and counsel each other, in order that they might grow as individuals and together. That's what marriage is intended to be. It is covenant. It is companionship.

Recently I read a beautiful description of this kind of marital companionship in a most unexpected place—*Esquire* magazine, which is not usually the source for illustration of marital bliss! Author Irwin Shaw described his marriage in the following terms: "Mutual and unexpressed understanding, private jokes, comfort in adversity, automatic support in times of trouble, and hours spent in cordial silence and tranquil evenings."[32]

I'm sure that many people read those words wistfully, wondering what happened to their marriages, which are so lacking in anything remotely like this kind of companionship. It could be that they never understood that marriages, like friendships, require work. Marriage companionship, like lasting friendship, takes time over the years to develop.

Marriage as Commitment
The fifth chapter of Proverbs contains unambiguous wisdom—values—for people who find themselves in tempting situations. And who doesn't in this world?

> *Keep to a path far from her,*
> *do not go near the door of her house,*
> *lest you give your best strength to others*
> *and your years to one who is cruel,*
> *lest strangers feast on your wealth*
> *and your toil enrich another man's house.*
> PROVERBS 5:8-10

If I didn't know better, I would think that the author of these proverbs had gone through the American divorce courts, where he came up against a slick attorney who took him to the cleaners! It sounds as if he endured the kind of situation where a man goes through a divorce, loses home and family, and drives to work past his old home each morning, where his former wife is now living happily with her new husband. Gritting his teeth, he drives on to work to earn money so that a stranger can feast on his wealth, ruefully remembering that it was his own infidelity that drove his wife into the other man's arms and his wealth into another man's pocket.

Good advice comes in both negative and positive forms. We've seen the negative; now look at the positive:

> *Drink water from your own cistern,*
> *running water from your own well.*
> *Should your springs overflow in the streets,*
> *your streams of water in the public squares?*
> *Let them be yours alone,*
> *never to be shared with strangers.*
> *May your fountain be blessed,*
> *and may you rejoice in the wife of your youth.*
> PROVERBS 5:15-18

There is a very definite sense of commitment here. It's your own cistern, your own well. Let it be yours alone, never to be shared with strangers. May your fountain be blessed, and may you rejoice in the wife of your youth.

Marriage is covenant. Marriage is companionship. Marriage is commitment. Commitment establishes marital foundations, and it builds in its own limits. There's a commitment to a relationship into which nobody else is allowed to intrude. This intimacy is preserved by refusing to take it outside the limits of the marital relationship. And these limits are designed to create an area in which an extraordinarily loving commitment might be nurtured and nourished.

One lovely summer day Jill and I got up early to get our morning exercise. Jill walks two miles around our lake in a clockwise direction. I run around it twice in a counterclockwise direction. I suppose you could say that's a picture of our marriage; she walks and I run, and we go in opposite directions! But as I was running and saw her in the distance walking toward me I thought how special she is to me, and as I passed her I said, "I love you." It seemed perfectly appropriate. I kept running; she kept walking, but as I passed her the second time I added, "And I still love you!" She laughed and kept on walking. I laughed and kept on running, and nobody watching would have known our intimate secret, but they would have seen two happy people enjoying each other. For forty-plus years that has been the basis of our marriage.

We noted some of the less-than-acceptable attitudes toward marriage that are being voiced and demonstrated by many of our celebrities. In all fairness, we need to note that there are glowing exceptions. Actor Paul Newman is one. Somewhere I came across this statement he made on the sixtieth birthday of his wife, Joanne Woodward, after they had been married thirty-two years:

> I feel privileged to love that woman. The fact that I am
> married to her is the single greatest joy of my life.
> Joanne is fascinating to me, and always will be. We live
> in a throwaway society. We throw away bottles and
> cans, children, careers and marriages. Joanne and I work
> at mending things. We fix the toaster when it breaks,
> and likewise we fix our marriage when it is strained.

This from a man surrounded by Hollywood's beautiful young things, rich and powerful, attractive and highly successful. Yet he says that his marriage to a sixty-year-old woman is "the single greatest joy of my life"! So all is not lost.

It is one thing to decide to get married. It is an entirely different matter to decide from the beginning that you intend to stay married.

It is quite easy to stand at the front of a church and make promises. It is another matter entirely to stick with the promises. In case I am talking to someone who was not paying attention on his or her wedding day, let me remind you that you promised to keep yourself for your spouse in a variety of circumstances covering the possibility of "sickness or health," "riches or poverty" and "better or worse." Granted, the old English may have been somewhat misleading and the emotion of the moment may have clouded your understanding, but who can possibly miss the point that in the marriage service we promise ourselves to each other in faithful commitment, whatever may happen during the course of marriage—whether physically, socially, emotionally, financially, or spiritually?

When people have complained to me about their marriage partners, I have often asked them how they came to be married to such undesirable people. Did someone hold a gun to their heads at the altar? Were they delivered to the church in a straitjacket in an armored car and escorted away with men brandishing Uzis? Of course not! They made a decision and freely chose to be married. So now they can decide to be faithful and that is precisely what God expects. It is in this kind of loving, committed relationship lived out God's way that lasting fulfillment is found.

In my pastoral ministry I have listened to many sad stories of marital unfaithfulness, abuse, neglect, and dysfunction. Often the subject has been raised by people who are seriously contemplating divorce as a solution to their marital problems, but unsure—sometimes because of a religious upbringing from which they strayed—whether they have the freedom to pursue such a course. So they ask the oft-asked question, "What does the Bible say about divorce?" My response over many years has been, "I'll tell you that if you first tell me what it says about marriage." And the answer almost invariably has been, "I really don't know what the Bible says about marriage." Therein lies the problem.

If you're married, take your marriage seriously. It's a precious thing, a major element in the life you live and, accordingly, a prime ingredient in the kind of person you are. And take some time to think carefully about the principles outlined in this chapter.

The social arrangement that has proved most successful in ensuring the
physical survival and promoting the social development of the child
is the family unit of the biological mother and father.
BARBARA DAFOE WHITEHEAD

A teenage son and his father were having a difference of
opinion. In exasperation the boy exploded, "I didn't ask to
be born into this family!" To which his father replied, "You're right,
and if you had, the answer would have been no!" On reflection, the
father might have modified his response, but there was no need for
the boy to alter his position—although his attitude could have been
improved!

Children are born, not because of their own desire, but because of
the action of their parents. This clearly places maximum responsibility for the child's well-being on those whose actions, from a human
point of view, brought about his or her existence.

IT TAKES ONE MAN AND ONE WOMAN TO MAKE ONE CHILD
Since a male and a female are necessary for producing the child, it
would seem logical that the male and female parents would accept the
privilege and responsibility of caring for the child they have produced.

There are many wonderful parents who, for reasons outside their control, find themselves struggling to raise children on their own without the benefit of a spouse. My own father was brought up by his gentle, sweet mother and his strong grandmother after his father died. And some of the most impressive young people I know are those who have been deserted by their former spouses and left to bring up children, often without even receiving the financial support to which they are entitled.

With these exceptions in mind, it is still reasonable and logical to say that a child should ideally have a parent of each sex, joined in the commitment of marriage, who will devote themselves to bringing up the child they have produced together. As simple and obvious as this is, it is not a unanimous position in our culture.

Increasingly we are seeing gays and lesbians, in their struggle to have their lifestyles accepted as normative, insisting that they should have full rights to adopt children and that their arrangement should be recognized as a family structure. Many of them, like one lesbian couple, both of whom are officers on the Boston police force, are making great efforts to show that the children they are bringing up will in no way be jeopardized, except perhaps, in their opinion, by the "bigotry" of those who disagree with their point of view. In an effort to ensure that young people brought up by gay or lesbian couples will not be ridiculed by their school friends, the New York Education Authority went to great trouble to produce books for students showing that there are different kinds of "families" and that we should be understanding and accept them. So it is easy to see that what has been the obvious way of looking at family is not so obvious—or so simple—anymore.

President Lyndon B. Johnson, speaking at Howard University in 1965, said, "The family is a cornerstone of our society. More than any other force it shapes the attitudes, the hopes, the ambitions, and the values of the child. When the family collapses, it is the children that are usually damaged. When it happens on a massive scale, the community itself is crippled." More recently Hillary Rodham Clinton wrote a popular book entitled *It Takes a Village,* which according to her supporters developed the theme that we, as a society, need to cooperate in raising our precious children, but which her detractors decried as a thinly veiled move to get "Big Government" involved in raising our kids! Whoever was right about the First Lady's intentions, she certainly raised the issue of child rearing as a top priority.

At first sight, President Johnson's quotation and Hillary Clinton's emphasis should encourage us, because they suggest that Washington is aware of the problem, is firmly on the side of the family, and will presumably come up with some solutions. But look again. Such is the struggle in high places on this subject that when the Carter administration called a White House conference on families in 1980, they achieved very little because the time was spent quarreling over what exactly constitutes a family! Those who assumed that they were going to discuss ways of helping Mom and Dad cope with the pressures of bringing up Johnny and Jenny in their home in the suburbs, while caring for a dog and a cat, were in for a rude awakening. To their horror and amazement, they found themselves confronted by groups of outspoken people who insisted on a new definition of "family," one that would not only recognize their particular brand of cohabitation as both common and normative, but would also give "nontraditional families" equal status with the "traditional family." Those who were surprised and dismayed were dismissed as zealots and bigots.

Barbara Dafoe Whitehead, in a startling article in *Atlantic Monthly,* wrote, "Every time the issue of family structure has been raised the response has been first controversy, then retreat, and finally silence." Wading into the controversy, armed with a mass of evidence from social science research, Whitehead took on the nay-sayers:

> The human child is born in an abjectly helpless and
> immature state. Years of nurture and protection
> are needed before the child can achieve physical

independence. Similarly, it takes years of interaction with at least one but ideally two or more adults for a child to develop into a socially competent adult. . . . The social arrangement that has proved most successful in ensuring the physical survival and promoting the social development of the child is the family unit of the biological mother and father.[33]

While Ms. Whitehead limited her remarks to the physical and social realms, the same things could be said about the child's spiritual well-being. So while in Washington the politicians may not have the nerve to address the issue of family structure, even though they are greatly concerned about the social and economic ramifications of family disintegration, there is no reason for Christians to retreat or remain silent, because the Scriptures are loud and clear on the subject.

PROVERBS ON THE FAMILY

As we look into the Scriptures we can discover not only what the issues are when we confront those who no longer accept what the Bible teaches on the family, but we will also be clear in our minds what family values are, particularly as they relate to bringing up children in a confused environment. Once again we will turn to the book of Proverbs.

Train a child in the way he should go,
and when he is old he will not turn from it.
PROVERBS 22:6

Some people take this as a cast-iron promise. They reason, "God says if I raise my kids as they ought to be raised, while they might deviate from my principles for a period, in the end they'll come around to the way I brought them up, and all will be well." This understanding has brought a considerable amount of comfort to godly parents who have watched their youngsters go off to college and go off the rails at the same time. But they have held on to the promise even when their children, who are no longer kids, persist in behavior patterns that are far removed from those they learned at their mother's knee.

No, there is no written guarantee here that the children of godly parents will always turn out to be godly. The facts clearly point in a different direction, and hard as it is for some of us to accept, this is not a promise; it is a proverb. Proverbs are pithy sayings that are generally true. For example, "Like father, like son" is generally true, but all of us know exceptions. "Forewarned is forearmed" is often very true, but there are too many examples of the forewarned who chose not to be forearmed. What then is the value of the statement, "Train a child in the way he should go, and when he is old he will not turn from it"? It is a proverb that states a general principle.

WHO DECIDES THE "SHOULD"?

"Should" is the operative word here. It is all about the way a child *should* go! But who decides the "should" for a child?

We might name the parents as those who set the direction for their child. And many parents do determine what their kids should be and what they should do. They feel that these children have been placed in their orbit of influence, that they are going to care for these children, and that part of that care is helping the child find a direction and assisting them on their way.

The book of Proverbs assumes that godly parents will endeavor to bring up godly children. But there are parents who go far beyond the designs of godliness for their children. Some put great pressure on their youngsters concerning where they should live and the details of their lifestyle. Some parents decide that their children should go to a particular school. In England (and here in America, too, I'm told) some parents sign their child up for entry into the school they themselves attended—as soon as the child is born! If the question is asked, "Why this school?" the only reason is, "Because that's the school I went to." Some people decide that their children should go into a certain career.

The reason? Because the family has been in this particular business for years, and the tradition must be carried on, or because the father has invested his life in creating the business, and he wants nothing more than to bequeath it to his children. My father worked very hard to build up a grocery business during the Depression and World War II years in Britain, and he wanted me to take over the business. But I had no interest and less desire, and he, fortunately, did not attempt to determine the "should" for me based on his own desires.

Sometimes there's a more subtle motivation. Parents have been known to steer their children in a certain direction because they were never allowed to go that way themselves. For years they have been resentful that they missed their life's dream, and they are determined that their children get the chance that they missed—whether the children want it or not. This kind of drive in the parent often hurts more than it helps in the development of that child.

I have a friend whose father was a successful dentist, so the son gained the impression that he should be a dentist, and for years he was a good one if not a very happy one. But he eventually sold his dental practice and became a landscape gardener, and he has never been more fulfilled. My daughter was convinced that I wanted her to be a surgeon, and so she applied herself assiduously to her pre-med studies, winning the prize for top student in her university during her junior year. But she was never comfortable with the peculiar pressures that medicine places on women who want to be wives and mothers as well as professionals. Actually, I had no such aspirations for her, and it was only after she became ill with anorexia nervosa that we discovered the misunderstanding and relieved the pressure. She went on to be a very fulfilled young Ph.D. in a totally different discipline, as well as a wife and mother.

Who then determines the "should"? If it isn't the parent, is it the child? Anyone who knows anything about children knows that they rarely know what they want to be when they grow up, even though well-meaning grown-ups insist on asking them. My wife, Jill, was eating dinner with a couple she had known since they were teenagers and was enjoying getting to know their children. The youngest was not getting a word in edgewise, so Jill asked him the inevitable question: "And what do you want to be when you grow up?" He was momentarily overwhelmed at being recognized, but after careful thought he said, "Bigger!" That's probably as far as most kids can safely project, although there are rare exceptions where youngsters know early on which way they want to go. But one can hardly leave young children alone to determine the "should" of their lives. If not the parents or the child, then who? That becomes the crucial question. Who determines the "should"?

HELPING YOUR CHILD DISCOVER GOD'S PLAN

We need to remember that Proverbs was written in the context of the covenant that God had established with his people, the people of Israel. The Lord had a plan for their lives. He had made that clear to Abraham and had reaffirmed it at regular intervals. It is clear that the Lord decided—and decides—the "should."

If that is the case, what is the role of the parent? The task of the parent is to embark, with the child, on an exploration of what God had in mind when he brought that child into the world and gave him to the parents to bring up.

In times of war naval vessels sometimes set out to sea without anyone on board having a clear idea of where they are going. For security reasons, the captain has instructions to proceed to a certain point without any details of final destination or assignment. When they reach that point, he and the first officer go to the ship's safe, and together they take out the sealed envelope in which the details of their mission are outlined. They had sailed from port under what are known as "sealed orders." The mission had already been determined, but they only discovered it after they had set sail.

I believe that children sail into life under sealed orders. The task of the parent, along with the child, is to break the seal and find out what God had in mind when he brought this child into existence. Together, parent and child discover the "should."

The question is, How do parents go about this high-sounding task?

The Power of Dedicating Your Child to the Lord

It is helpful to notice that the word "train" can also mean "dedicate" or "inaugurate." In the same way that buildings are dedicated or inaugurated when they are completed and ready for occupancy, so parents set the child on the right course, inaugurating the process of discovering and doing God's will. If a child is dedicated to the Lord and the parents are dedicated to bringing that child up to be what he or she was dedicated to be, then they can discover together the "should" that God has in mind for the child. The child who has been told that the parents have committed themselves to discovering God's plans for him or her is likely to become intrigued by that thought and grow interested in joining the adventure.

Recently I received a copy of a book called *In the Heart of Savgedom* by Eva Stuart Watt. I had been looking for a copy for many years, because shortly before I was born my father was reading this book, which tells the story of Eva's and her family's incredibly courageous missionary ventures more than a hundred years ago into what they called "the heart of savagedom"—in what we now call Zaire. My father was so impressed by the Stuart Watt family that he looked up from his reading and said to my mother, who was about to produce me, "If this child's a boy, his name is Stuart!"

I was so pleased to receive my copy of the book because it allowed me to see for myself what had impressed my father so much that he had wanted to dedicate me to its message. It was all about ministry and mission! So every time I think about how I got my name, I think of missions and ministry. It is not really surprising that I turned out the way that I did! Of course, there is no guarantee that dedicating a child will always bring this sort of result. But this kind of action on the part of a parent, along with the work of God's grace, will have a profound, positive effect on a child. "Train a child in the way he should go, and when he is old he will not turn from it" is a rule that is generally true. That's one reason we teach values to our children.

Setting a Course to a Good Destination
The prologue to the book of Proverbs says:

> *[Proverbs are] for giving prudence to the simple,*
> *knowledge and discretion to the young.*
> PROVERBS 1:4

We've already looked into these words *knowledge* and *discretion*. Together they mean developing perceptive, workable plans for life. Assuming that children are being steered in the way that they should go, they then need help getting there. It's one thing to help a young person discover God's purpose, but it's an entirely different thing to help him put it into practice. It is not uncommon for young people to have a theoretical concept of the divine will but to be sadly deficient in know-how as to what it looks like or how it works. Parents can help by modeling this process in their own lives and by surrounding the child with other positive role models. As I look back on my early childhood, there's absolutely no question in my mind that I am, to a very large extent, a reflection of the role models who surrounded me. These people were both interesting and attractive to me.

I think particularly of Captain Horace Sidney May of the Royal Artillery. He was every inch a soldier, unabashedly a Christian, helpful, friendly, cheerful, positive, open, interested in me—everything I thought a man should be! Long after I left England, he still wrote to me regularly in impeccable handwriting—something he modeled that I have not emulated. His letters were invariably full of joy, brimming with vision, always positively looking for ways to make his life count for God. He told me he listened regularly to my radio broadcasts, and he frequently made suggestions about how they could be improved—and occasionally put my theology straight! He died a few years ago, in his nineties. Even though I hadn't seen him for years, I experienced a deep sense of loss at his passing. Part of my life had passed on too.

I think of Harry Green. He was a jovial bank manager. He steered me in the direction of a banking career, which I followed for twelve years. From him I learned that you could be an outspoken, outgoing Christian and a well-respected, highly efficient, thoroughly decent businessman. After I saw him in action, I knew that I wanted to be like him.

You see, the task of the parent is to instill into the child both by verbal teaching and by positive models workable ways of getting where Junior is supposed to be. That is the task and the responsibility of parents.

Giving Instruction on How to Live with Others

Listen, my son, to your father's instruction,
and do not forsake your mother's teaching.
They will be a garland to grace your head
and a chain to adorn your neck.
PROVERBS 1:8-9

Father and mother, both of whom are involved in training and instructing the child, are doing so in order that the child may develop a life "adorned" with gracious behavior. It is nice to meet well-behaved kids. It is not a nice experience to meet brats who are an utter pain to themselves and everybody who has the misfortune of crossing their paths.

Now I am not suggesting goody-two-shoes little kids. I like precocious, lively kids—kids who are pushing the limits, not because they have a rebellious spirit, but because they have a healthy spirit of adventure and discovery. I have three of my own, who are now busy producing—at a phenomenal rate—grandchildren of a similar disposition.

I got a great charge out of a kid who came to me one Sunday morning between services and said, "Well, Stuart, have you got anything significant to say this morning?" I knew exactly what his parents had been talking about in the car on the way to church!

One lovely summer's evening I was sitting at a Milwaukee Brewers baseball game across the aisle from a young family. The little boy was obnoxious. His parents were oblivious. He was unruly and rude, blocking people's vision, refusing to sit down when asked, and generally making a nuisance of himself. All the time his parents acted as if he were on another planet. Perhaps they wished he were! At one point he threw some popcorn over the man sitting behind him, who had been trying to get the boy to sit down. The man turned to the little boy and said, "How old are you, son?"

The boy replied, "I'm seven. Who wants to know?"

The man responded with gritted teeth, "Would you like to see eight?"

And I said, "Hallelujah!"

That little kid needed some major help, and he was getting absolutely none from his parents. They were producing, by negligence, a kid who was going to be a drag on society. We teach values to our children in order that, having ingrained them into their lives, they will become a garland to grace their head and a chain to adorn their neck.

Being an Involved Parent

My son, if you accept my words
and store up my commands within you,
turning your ear to wisdom

and applying your heart to understanding,
and if you call out for insight
and cry aloud for understanding,
and if you look for it as for silver
and search for it as for hidden treasure,
then you will understand the fear of the LORD
and find the knowledge of God.

PROVERBS 2:1-5

This is a parent addressing a young person on such significant topics as the fear of the Lord and the knowledge of God. In other words, here we have a parent teaching values—deep, spiritual realities.

One of the encouraging aspects of the Boomer generation is that many of them, having adopted a certain lifestyle in the turbulent sixties, have decided they don't want their children to emulate their example. I remember one definition of a conservative: "a liberal with teenage daughters"! Many baby boomers are returning to the church in order to give their children some moral teaching. This is good. But all too often they simply hand over their children to the professionals at church to provide for their spiritual needs in much the same way that they hand over their children to professional teachers to meet their educational needs and to the doctor to fix their physical problems.

This approach has a certain logic, but it is inadequate from a spiritual perspective. By all means, parents should utilize the church's ministries as a supplement to their own teaching at home—but not as a substitute for parental spiritual input. The church's ministry is a supplement, not a substitute.

Some years ago a popular song contained the helpful advice, "Don't send your kids to Sunday school; get out of bed and take 'em." If parents want their children to take spiritual matters seriously, they must make spiritual matters a priority in their *own* lives. Young people have an unerring sense of justice and uprightness, particularly when it comes to the way their parents treat them. They can smell inconsistency and hypocrisy a mile away and ferret it out with disconcerting skill. If kids know that Mom and Dad drop them off at Sunday school and then go off to drink coffee, they are quick to recognize the double standard. If the kids observe that their family worships only when there is nothing more exciting to do, guess what? They decide that worship is not very important. Kids who never see their parents pray and never hear their parents read from God's Word find it hard to believe that prayer and Scripture are indispensable ingredients to balanced living. Wise parents know that if their children are to be what they were created to be they need consistent and constant spiritual oversight and encouragement at home.

SETTING FAMILY GUIDELINES
Parenting with consistency can be such a challenging task that we err either by giving up on enforcing any rules or by burdening our children with far more rules than are necessary. When our three children were young, we adopted some basic principles concerning their spiritual development.

Briscoe Family Guideline #1: This family believes in and practices daily devotions.
There were times when we tried to have family devotions together. When the children were young it worked reasonably well, depending on how interesting we made the exercise. But once the children were adolescents, it became increasingly difficult to get everyone in the same place at the same time. Eventually we came to the conclusion that we shouldn't push it if it didn't work. Why frustrate everyone in the name of worship? So to each child we gave devotional materials appropriate to his or her interests at the time, and we encouraged them to spend a few minutes in their own devotions every day. We

kept an eye on them, assisting them as necessary. And it worked very well most of the time.

Briscoe Family Guideline #2: This family worships in church regularly.

We told our children, "Sunday mornings are for worship." Then we amplified the rule: "Wherever you are, whatever you're doing, whoever you're with, whatever your circumstances might be, Sunday morning is for worship, end of discussion." There were, of course, rare exceptions like fatal illness! Sunday evening services were optional. The option worked as follows: "If you can think of a valid reason you should not participate, then tell us about it, and we'll decide if it is valid or not." We retained parental authority but gave them a degree of freedom, and it taught them that freedom must be handled responsibly. In fact, it was a non-issue because most of their friends worshiped on Sunday evenings, and they wanted to be with their friends. Peer pressure at that stage of the game was more significant than parental pressure. That is why wise parents expose their children to healthy, positive peer pressure whenever possible.

Briscoe Family Guideline #3: Members of this family will engage in at least one midweek spiritual activity of their choice.

Each of our children chose entirely different activities, but while we made the rule, they made the choices—and stuck with them. When they were out on their own, they would make their own choices about spiritual involvement, but until that time, we as parents were seriously endeavoring to teach them how to be and do what God wanted them to be and do.

Children habitually "kick against the goads" of much that their parents do, but wise parents accept this temporary unpleasantness as par for the course, knowing full well that if they lead their children to discover and do the "should," there is a reasonable chance they will, in time, rise up and call their parents blessed.

THE PARENT'S ULTIMATE RESPONSIBILITY

Parents have been given an awesome task. If we are going to invest ourselves in our children, we're going to do it by training them in the way they should go, according to divine dictates, by developing practical ways of getting them there, by teaching them behaviors that will adorn their lives with a gracious lifestyle, so that they might discover spiritual realities and avoid destructive behaviors. These are the concerns of a parent who takes parenting seriously.

What kind of learning environment do we need for the kind of development I've just described? Allow me to use a very simple acrostic based on the word CHILD that will give us five ingredients necessary for producing an environment in which spiritual learning can take place.

Character
Harmony
Instruction
Love
Discipline

Character

I grew up in Britain during World War II. The bombs were falling on us regularly. We would wake up to find entire blocks of houses gone and classmates dead. It was not a secure world for kids trying to grow up, but I remember feeling quite secure. Why? My parents gave me the sense that God would take care of whatever we had entrusted to him. The faith of my father and mother offered me stability in a frightening, shifting world.

Children are sensitive to the character of their parents. They pick up peace or fear, anger or happiness. And they can withstand a lot of pressure and trial from outside if the home inside is held steady by parents whose character is steady and consistent.

Harmony

We don't need studies to prove to us the damage being done to children by the trauma of divorce. But we might be surprised to learn that children are often seriously damaged by strife in the home, even when divorce does not occur. It is the responsibility of parents to work out their conflicts for the sake of the children as well as themselves. Children growing up in turmoil will suffer and be hindered in their spiritual, emotional, mental, and even physical growth. Disagreements between parents are to be expected unless one of them has stopped thinking! But kids are quick to capitalize on any perceived crack in the solidarity of parents. It is therefore imperative that any area of discussion or disagreement be handled with great care—and often out of earshot of the kids!

Instruction

> *The wise in heart are called discerning,*
> *and pleasant words promote instruction.*
> PROVERBS 16:21

Children love to learn—they have a built-in desire to accomplish new tasks and gain new skills—but they don't learn well in the midst of criticism and tension. Make learning pleasant as well as instructive for your children. This is part of your task, and it can be one of the most rewarding parts, as you see that son or daughter gain wisdom and apply skill to everyday life. All a parent needs to do is to imagine that their boss talks to them the way they talk to their kids. The boss who continually berates, criticizes, and demeans does not produce a happy worker. And the employer who never rewards, rarely encourages, is stinting in his praise, and never thinks to give credit where it is due will produce a surly employee. In the same way kids are people who hurt, get upset, need encouragement, respond to praise, and love incentives. The wise parent knows this and makes the learning process as pleasant as possible. Charles Haddon Spurgeon, the great preacher, used to tell his students, "Pleasantly profitable let all our preaching be." Wise parents take a leaf out of the preacher's book!

Love

> *Let love and faithfulness never leave you;*
> *bind them around your neck,*
> *write them on the tablet of your heart.*
> PROVERBS 3:3

When we forget the meaning of love, 1 Corinthians 13 will refresh our memory. An environment that encourages the development of healthy kids has a healthy atmosphere of love—kindness, forgiveness, honesty, and patience.

Discipline

Discipline goes hand in hand with love; one is not complete without the other. Not to discipline your child is a dreadfully unloving thing to do. But how we discipline each individual child varies according to their and our temperaments. Our children need to learn boundaries early. They need to see that actions have consequences and that they don't always get what they want or even what is fair. They need to learn how to treat others with respect—and all of this begins at home.

Is there any guarantee that if we do everything right, our children will turn out all right? I don't believe so. There is too much evidence to the contrary—perfectly good parents have produced kids who are in deep, deep trouble, and perfectly *awful* parents have produced wonderful kids.

My wife, Jill, sometimes reminds me that God had two children, whom he put in Paradise with very simple and straightforward rules—and they still went wrong. Our children will make their own choices. Our responsibility is to do all we can according to the principles our Lord has given us. In our parenting God never called us to be perfect; he called us to be faithful. Faithful parents know how to make good choices for their children and make wise decisions about how their children will be raised.

There's no question about it, the sex-related issues are going to be the
most important issues facing all churches in the foreseeable future.
Abortion, AIDS, premarital sex, homosexuality,
all those are going to be at the vortex.

GEORGE GALLUP

*R*ecently, as I was driving to Chicago to speak at a fund-raising
banquet for a crisis pregnancy center, I had the opportunity
to listen to afternoon radio, a rare experience for me. I tuned in to a
call-in show, on which a doctor was dispensing medical advice. The
first question came from a young lady who wanted to get pregnant
through artificial insemination. She was concerned because the proposed donor of the sperm was an alcoholic. She wanted to know if her
baby would inherit alcoholic tendencies. The doctor asked why she
wanted to be artificially inseminated. He said, "Is your partner unable
to impregnate you?" She replied, "Yes, she's female." Barely missing a
beat, the doctor responded a tad lamely, "Oh, I see." Further conversation revolved around complications that might arise because the
proposed donor was the brother of her companion.

The next caller wanted to know if it is possible to contract AIDS
through the sperm of a partner who has AIDS and has impregnated
you. This led to further questions as to whether there is more danger of
catching AIDS through sexual contact alone or through pregnancy.

This enlightening conversation was followed by another questioner anxious to know more about fetal tissue research and what it could do to alleviate Alzheimer's and Parkinson's. What did the doctor think about harvesting cells from the fetuses of elective abortions for the purposes of such research?

Each of these discussions went on for some time, and I wondered if George Gallup was listening. If so, he probably was not as surprised as I was, because he had said that the most important issues out there are abortion, AIDS, premarital sex, and homosexuality. It struck me that the first three questions on that afternoon's call-in show on one of Milwaukee's top radio stations dealt with abortion, AIDS, and homosexuality.

After such heavy subjects we were in for a surprise. The next caller asked about acne. I don't ever remember feeling so relieved to hear a discussion of pimples. As the doctor droned on, discussing the perils of acne in a tone of voice no different from that with which he had intoned advice on abortion, homosexuality, and AIDS, I realized that nobody had asked about premarital sex, which figured on Mr. Gallup's list. But I didn't have to wait long.

The next program was introduced by the host saying, "Today we're going to discuss the high school student who was chosen by her peers to be homecoming queen." Immediately I knew which high school student he wanted to discuss—the one who was pregnant! When it was discovered that she was pregnant, the administration decided that they did not want her to be homecoming queen. She was not, in their opinion, a suitable role model for other students. So they rigged the election, covered it up, and the first runner-up was crowned. Somebody, however, spilled the beans, and the school officials were fired and the pregnant queen crowned. Considerable outrage was leveled at the administrators, who had taken it upon themselves to decide who could and could not be homecoming queen and who thought they had the right to decide who was or was not a suitable role model. This issue filled another half hour of prime time radio without difficulty. It also provided the last item of Mr. Gallup's list; premarital sex took its place alongside AIDS, homosexuality, and abortion as suitable fare for afternoon easy listening.

To say that we live in a sex-saturated society is to be guilty of stating the obvious. But sometimes we can be so blinded by the obvious that we don't recognize the environment in which we're living. We are like city dwellers who have become so accustomed to smog that they are unaware of the condition of their lungs.

How Did We Come to This?

We can't continue this discussion without remembering something called the "sexual revolution." It reached its peak in those exciting, troubling days called "the sixties." Those were the days when thousands of young people rebelled against most things that their parents stood for—with the possible exception of plastic credit cards—and enjoyed themselves at events like Woodstock. This was a musical event where hundreds of thousands of our brightest and best sang songs of love and peace, sated themselves with uninhibited sex, stoned themselves out of their minds on grass and acid, and slithered in sloppy mud, garlanded in flowers and nothing much else.

As I write these words more than thirty years later, many of those young people have grown up to be respectable citizens who listen to music more extreme, do drugs but call them "recreational," and cavort in hot tubs rather than cold mud while finding ways to enjoy "safe sex." And they have raised kids who, in large measure, have followed the only role models they had—either their parents or their heroes on entertainment screens or playing fields. And that's how we got where we are.

It would be a mistake to assume that this sexual revolution actually changed sexual behavior. There have always been all kinds of sexual activity, abuse, and aberrations. If you are in any doubt, read the Old Testament; they are all enumerated there quite plainly.

So if behavior didn't change, how could there have been a "revolution"? It was not so much that sexual *activities* changed, but that *attitudes* toward the activities changed. There was a time when people, deep down, believed that there was a God who had certain standards. He said, among other things, "You shall not commit adultery," and "You shall not covet your neighbor's wife." This didn't necessarily stop them from doing what he had forbidden, but if they did it, they felt that they had done something wrong. So they acted clandestinely. They had to deal with guilt and shame. There was no shortage of shameful activity going on, but at least people had the grace to be ashamed. They had the sense to believe that they were contravening some standards.

But when the sexual revolution came along, instead of being shamed by an educated conscience or having shame placed upon them by society, people were affirmed in their needs and feelings and encouraged to do what felt good to them and applauded for doing it. Behavior that used to be covert became overt. Historical Judeo-Christian standards of sexual morality were either blandly ignored or boldly repudiated. As a result sexual impropriety became more commonplace and its negative consequences more widespread.

From Absolute to Relative

Attitudes toward "absolute" and "relative" values have changed drastically. There has been a great move away from any sense of sexual absolutes. In the place of a God in whom moral righteousness is found and in obedience to whose principles a morally upright life can be lived, autonomous humankind was crowned—humans who knew better than God how to behave sexually. As God fell out of favor and his righteousness took a tumble, so man took the place of God and decided that what had been regarded previously as naughty was actually nice and what had been off-limits was now mainstream. From now on, man would determine for himself what was good and right and true. The net result, of course, is that all kinds of behaviors have become socially acceptable. People now say, "Nobody has the right to tell anybody else what is right or wrong. If it is right for you, then it is right."

This is all very high sounding. What could be more adult and mature than the ability to recognize that you don't know everything, that you may be wrong, that other people are as smart or smarter than you are, and that, therefore, the only appropriate way to look at anything is to see it through the lenses of toleration?

Charles Colson wrote the following:

> The only stable value left in this relativistic world is unbridled tolerance. The modern broadmindedness purports that any and all values, if sincerely held, are equally valid.[34]

It is not difficult to see that this is a major departure from what the Christian church has believed throughout history. Christians do not accept that all standards, if sincerely held, are of equal value. We believe that a person can be sincerely wrong. If there is such a thing as truth, there must, by definition, be something called error. If it is possible to be right, it must be equally possible to be wrong!

From Fear to Freedom

There has also been a shift from an attitude of fear to one of freedom. Part of our problem is that puberty seems to be happening earlier, and people are getting married later, which means that there is a longer period during which the sexual appetites of young people are developing but cannot be fulfilled legitimately according to Christian teaching. So there is a long, painful period when youngsters are struggling with their sexuality.

When I was in youth ministry (slightly after the medieval period), we found it necessary to talk to young people about sex. In those days our approach was less than sophisticated. We taught them what the Bible says about sex, but we also worked hard to put the fear of the living God in them. We told them about "the three fears": the fear of infection, the fear of conception, and the fear of detection. The fear of infection, stated simply, was, "You don't want to have sex—you could catch a social disease." That's what we called them in those days—"social diseases"—and we never mentioned them by name. This was the fear of infection.

Then we used to tell them, "Listen, you could get pregnant, and then you really would be in a mess. What in the world would you say to your parents? What would they think in your school?" This was the fear of conception approach. Now kids can get an abortion without telling their parents, even though they can't have their ears pierced without parental permission! And their schools are so understanding that they will arrange babysitting for the children of the children who graduated to parenthood before graduating from high school.

Warming to our theme, we told the young people of yesteryear, "If you have sex with your boyfriend before you get married, somebody might find out!"—the fear of detection. So the fears of infection, conception, and detection, to a large extent, scared the kids off.

But of course things have changed. Now if you talk to kids about the fear of infection, they look at you as if you just crawled out from under a rock, and they'll bring you up to date on the modern drugs that will handle STDs, which they don't think they will catch anyway. AIDS does scare them a little, but not enough, because they've been indoctrinated about "safe sex," even if they more often than not do not practice what is preached (and because "safe sex" really isn't).

As far as fear of detection is concerned, in their opinion that is a "no-brainer." To them it's nobody else's business what you do with your own body. And if anyone objects to your sexual behavior, you can tell him, "Up your nose! Who cares about what you think?" They take comfort in the belief that all those who complain about the decline in sexual mores are probably frigid and frustrated at best or card-carrying hypocrites at worst.

As far as fear of conception is concerned, if one is unlucky enough to conceive, then of course the ultimate contraceptive, abortion, is available on demand. So now the message our youth believe and propagate to each other is, "Don't worry about infection, don't worry about conception, and don't worry about detection. Be free. Don't fear."

Now I will be the first to admit that our old "fear" approach was as subtle as a sledgehammer, but I'm afraid the new "freedom" approach has all the subtlety of the serpent. In matters as deadly—and I mean deadly—as sexual promiscuity, I prefer sledgehammers to serpents.

From Being Good to Feeling Good
There was a time when people grew up with the desire to be good and to do things that were good. When Queen Victoria was eleven years old, her governess showed her a list of the British kings and queens, with her name at the bottom of the list. The child burst into tears, then, drying her eyes, stood up and said, "I *will* be good!" Skeptics would call that kind of attitude positively Victorian! Nowadays she would be surrounded by television crews with reporters sticking microphones under her eleven-year-old chin asking, "Do you feel good about being queen one day, Vicky?" Queen Victoria lived in a day when, even though she did not *feel* good about the burdens of royalty, she nevertheless accepted the duties her position had laid upon her—including the duty to *be* good. How old-fashioned this sounds!

Modern culture tends to disparage being good and frequently derides good people as "do-gooders." To call somebody a do-gooder is an insult. The question is no longer, "Are there good things that I should do and bad things that I should avoid?" The question now is, "What can I do that will make me feel good?" Whether it is good or bad is a matter of fundamental indifference. And if you don't feel good about what you're doing, then you can always get therapy—therapy that all too often helps people feel good about being bad. This is the way things have progressed—or rather, regressed.

There's nothing completely new about this. Ernest Hemingway said, "What is moral is what you feel good after, and what is immoral is what you feel bad after."[35] The fact that he eventually killed himself suggests that he finished up feeling as bad as it is possible to feel, and by his own definition his life must have been deeply immoral.

From Commitment to Enjoyment

When Christians speak out on matters of sexual morality, people think that they, and therefore God, are against sex. Yet the Bible insists that God himself thought the first thought about sex. It was God who made male and female for rather obvious reasons. It was he who insisted that people should enjoy sex as an expression of their love and faithfulness. It was his idea that through sex they should produce and then bring up children in the nurture and admonition of the Lord. That is exactly what the Bible teaches about sex in the context of commitment. Somewhere along the line the idea crept in that commitment is the enemy of enjoyment. So it is no surprise that commitment is what people don't want anymore; it is too confining.

Book clubs used to offer free books on the condition that a commitment was made to purchase at least four more books in the following two years. Now they simply offer free books with no strings attached. "No commitment required," they advertise, plastering magazines with our culture's dominant theme! Without commitment, enrollment has boomed. With mandatory commitment, it was a bust—because people are looking for enjoyment without commitment, even in the purchase of books!

In the same way, if it is possible for people to have the enjoyment of sex without the awkwardness and the challenge of commitment in which God intended the joy of sex to be experienced, so much the better, as far as they're concerned.

The net result of these dramatically changed attitudes is a decisively different atmosphere, an atmosphere in which the message of sex is trumpeted loudly from the rooftops. Sex is fun, sex is freedom, and sex is fulfillment. Tune in to talk shows, and you will find that the talk often has to do with sex. The more titillating the better. In fact, the producer of one of these shows said recently, "The problem that we're facing now is that there's tremendous competition to get the kind of people on our shows that are going to attract an audience. It used to be if we could get some prostitutes on to talk about being prostitutes, that would do it. But now we have to have prostitutes who love sex, or prostitutes whose fathers approve, because we have to keep ahead of the competition."

DAMAGE ASSESSMENT

Even Dear Abby, who over the years has dispensed a considerable amount of common sense and helpful advice, recently wrote, "Anything that goes on between consenting adults is okay as long as it is agreeable with both parties and harms no one." But former seminary president Robertson McQuilkin, commenting on Dear Abby's tolerant viewpoint, responded, "'Harms no one' is the key, but who but God knows how much harm is being done?" Exactly! Only God knows how much harm is being done in illicit sexual liaisons.

We can, however, do empirical research and make fairly accurate observations about the harm being done. For instance, Dr. Robert J. Collins published in the *Journal of the American Medical Association* the results of his research on young women attending Midwestern universities. He stated that 80 percent of the young women who had sex before marriage hoped that the premarital sex would lead to marriage with their sexual partner. Eighty percent of them! But only 12 percent of the men involved in the sexual activity had the same expectation. This suggests, once more, that men by nature tend to be more promiscuous and that women have a tendency toward monogamy. Given these widely divergent expectations, who is to say no harm is being done? If a young woman looking for love and commitment enters a sexual relationship only to be disappointed in her hopes, will there not be harm done to her? And the young man, having deceived the young woman and cheated her out of something precious, has damaged his own credibility and masculinity. The old adage says, "Men give intimacy to get sex, and women give sex to get intimacy." If there is any truth in that, you don't need to have a Ph.D. in psychology to see the possibilities for harm in premarital sexual relationships.

What about the harm done to spouses by cheating partners? Who can measure the sense of betrayal, who can calculate the weight of rejection, and who can plumb the depth of pain? Who knows the impact on the bewildered children, and who can calculate the cost of broken homes? Who can estimate the extent of corrupt modeling, and who dares attempt to understand the pain of a broken heart? While our culture trumpets the exhilarating gospel of free sex as fun and fulfilling, wiser heads shake with dissent, and tender hearts grieve for God's erring children.

One of the most remarkable changes in America's social mores in recent years has to do with changing attitudes toward smoking. Not too long ago cigarette smoking was portrayed on TV as the height of sophistication and an indispensable component of the "good life." Incredibly good-looking young women exuding health and sex appeal placed cigarettes elegantly between their ruby lips and, leaning back languidly, breathed out wreaths of smoke into the sultry evening air. Meanwhile, the Marlboro man, with jawline straight as an arrow and penetrating eyes, gazed from under the rim of his ten-gallon hat into a distance that hinted of adventure. These ads were selling lies.

Eventually people caught on as the consequences of smoking became clearer to the public. Instead of glamour pictures, someone produced pictures of ashtrays full of twisted, burned, stained, smelly butts. The Surgeon General successively added increasingly forthright warnings; the politicians added taxes; and slowly, ever so slowly, the mores changed. People got the message: We've been sold a bill of goods. Smoking is not what it was cracked up to be. Now you can't even smoke in many outdoor stadiums. Smoking is forbidden in airports, hospitals and many restaurants. People speak knowledgeably about secondhand smoke and they understand the relationship between smoking and cancer, blood pressure, and fetuses. What a turnaround!

I look for a similar turnaround in sexual attitudes. We need it desperately. But where to start? How about the NBA?

Tell me—what do Wilt Chamberlain, Magic Johnson, David Robinson, and A. C. Green have in common? Easy! They are all superb athletes who have starred in the National Basketball Association. What do they not have in common? Wilt Chamberlain and Magic Johnson have openly admitted to incredibly promiscuous sex lives, which in Magic's case has led to his contracting the HIV virus. But David Robinson and A. C. Green have made a rap tape about chastity! When A. C. was interviewed by Rush Limbaugh, the hyper-opinionated radio personality questioned his message. A. C. simply replied, "I am a virgin!" Limbaugh was finally silenced—a moment to be cherished in the history of radio. But why was Limbaugh silenced? Because it never occurred to him that a young athlete living in the "anything goes" atmosphere of the NBA, where young women make themselves readily available for sex, would choose to be sexually pure. But why would some go the way of a Robinson or a Green and others prefer the path of a Johnson or a Chamberlain? It's a matter of the moral principles they embraced.

NOTHING NEW UNDER THE MOON

Allow me to direct your attention once again to the book of Proverbs, specifically, to chapter 7. This chapter is unlike many of the other chapters in Proverbs in that it is not a list of apparently unrelated, succinct, pithy, proverbial sayings, but is a striking account of a sexual seduction. The story tells of a young man who goes out and is confronted by an experienced woman who leads him into a seductive situation. This is not an misogynistic story. More often than not, the sexual aggressor is the male. But in this instance an older woman takes the lead and with much skill offers a young man a tempting opportunity.

There's much that we can learn from this situation. You don't need a vivid imagination to picture the scene:

> *At the window of my house*
> *I looked out through the lattice.*
> *I saw among the simple,*
> *I noticed among the young men,*
> *a youth who lacked judgment. . . .*
> *Then out came a woman to meet him,*
> *dressed like a prostitute and with crafty intent.*
>
> PROVERBS 7:6-10

Notice three specific things:

- The vulnerability of the man.
- The availability of the woman.
- The desirability of sex.

Let me put three key words together and make a very simple equation for you.

Vulnerability + Availability + Desirability = Possibility

Possibility of what? The possibility of either doing right or going wrong. The four basketball stars I mentioned above have all been exposed to precisely the same kinds of situations. The difference, however, between their experiences is simply that two of them chose to do right and the other two preferred to go wrong. Every seductive situation offers the chance to go either way. What determines the difference? Decisions and the values upon which the decisions are based!

THE HEART IS A SEX ORGAN

Above all else, guard your heart,
for it is the wellspring of life.

PROVERBS 4:23

The young man in Proverbs 7 "lacked judgment"; literally, he was lacking in "heart." A biblical proverb is a statement concerning the truth that comes from God that we are to assimilate into our hearts. Truth assimilated then becomes the principle of operation, the standard of values, the grounds of decisions, the basis of lifestyle. The tragedy with the young man in the story was that he lacked heart. He had either missed out on discovering the principles that God has ordained for sexual behavior, or he thought that he knew better than God. What he lacked in heart, however, he more than made up in hormones, and as a result he was a sitting duck. What a sad picture of vulnerability he presents!

It is a pity that many people today are not only ignorant of biblical principles concerning their sexuality but are constantly exposed to contrary principles. They remind me of one of the most dangerous experiences of my life. As a young Marine, I joined a number of friends in a sailing expedition for which we were ill-equipped. As a result of our ineptitude, we managed to sail out of sight of land, and when we tried to bring the boat about, we only succeeded in breaking the mast and losing our sails. We then discovered that the tide had turned and was taking us even farther out to sea. So not only did we lack the power to go the right way, but even if we'd known which way was the right way—which we didn't—we were also subjected to powerful forces taking us the wrong way. We survived, but the survival had little to do with us. We were rescued by the coast guard and towed crestfallen back into port!

But let's get back to our young man. What happened to him?

He was going down the street near her corner,
walking along in the direction of her house
at twilight, as the day was fading,
as the dark of night set in.
PROVERBS 7:8-9

If this sounds vaguely ominous, it is. Lacking heart, he's heading in the wrong direction with nothing to hold him, nothing to stay his course.

One day an old gentleman noticed a little boy going round and round the block on his tricycle. This went on all morning, and finally the old man stopped the little boy and said, "Son, aren't you getting tired? You've being going round and round the block all morning."

The little boy replied, "I'm running away from home."

The old man responded, "You're not running away from home, son. You're just going round and round the block."

But the boy insisted, "No, I'm running away from home, but Mommy said I mustn't cross the road."

He was doing what many kids want to do at least once in their lives—run away from home. Fortunately, Mommy had built some boundaries into him. And those boundaries kept him from running into the street. At the moment of vulnerability there were limits that held him, even though he didn't want to be held!

But what happens to those who are heading in the wrong direction with nothing to hold them? In their vulnerability they usually meet up with availability dressed up in desirability. And how desirable it is!

Those people who say they can't understand the Bible should be made to read Proverbs 7. Language doesn't get much clearer than that.

MACHO MAN OR SITTING DUCK?

"She took hold of him and kissed him" (v. 13)—hardly the most subtle of approaches. "I looked for you and have found you!" she added (v. 15). This was heady stuff for a young man on the loose. Flattered, his sense of desirability massaged, his self-image inflated by her attention, what was there to hinder him from responding to her advances?

"Come, let's drink deep of love till morning; let's enjoy ourselves with love!" she said (v. 18). There was nothing complicated about her approach. She talked about love, but she wasn't interested in love. True love requires commitment and self-sacrifice. She talked of love, but she meant raw sex. And she talked of enjoyment, which was all the young man was looking for. Nothing like a little bit of fun!

Just in case, as a child of the covenant, he had any qualms about doing what the covenant forbade—that is, committing adultery—she told him, "I have fellowship offerings at home; today I fulfilled my vows" (v. 14). He shouldn't have any religious hang-ups, because she was religious, too. She had just come back from the worship center; she had fulfilled her religious obligations, and she had brought back some of the choice meat from her offerings, which meant that there was a steak dinner with the deal. So his conscience could be seared while his steak was grilled. What more could he possibly wish for? Oh, and by the way—her husband was going to be out of town on business for a few days, so there was no need to be afraid. The sex would be safe. No need to be upright and certainly no necessity to be uptight.

"With persuasive words she led him astray; she seduced him with her smooth talk" (v. 21). There is nothing much smoother than the modern offering of sex without shame, without limits, and without consequences.

But wait! What happened to our young buck?

All at once he followed her
like an ox going to the slaughter,
like a deer stepping into a noose
till an arrow pierces his liver,
like a bird darting into a snare,
little knowing it will cost him his life.

PROVERBS 7:22-23

There's great irony in the way this passage of Scripture ends. Picture the young man, hormones raging, pulse pounding, ego bursting, stepping out to capitalize on an offer that is too good to be true. He's at the top of his game. He's all man, and he's about to prove it. But from heaven's vantage point he looks more like an ox going to slaughter, a deer stepping into a noose, or a bird darting into a snare. He's thinking of freedom and fun, but he'll end up fettered by a desire for more and bored by the meaninglessness of his own gratification. Champagne in the evening and real pain in the morning. Or as Meryl Streep's character in the film *Postcards from the Edge* said with searing honesty: "I was into pain reduction and mind expansion, but what I've ended up with is pain expansion and mind reduction."

Her house is a highway to the grave,
leading down to the chambers of death.

PROVERBS 7:27

You may say, "That's a bit melodramatic, isn't it?" I don't think so. First, the Bible says, "The wages of sin is death" (Rom. 6:23). There are all kinds of sin, and sex outside of divinely ordained limits is one of them. Let's be clear about this: The wages of sin is death. So if we're engaging in illicit sex, we need to recognize that we are under the judgment of God, and we should come to repentance, faith, forgiveness, restoration, and newness of life in Christ—and live in purity.

The second thing to bear in mind is this: Dr. J. D. Unwin of Cambridge University studied eighty civilizations that span four thousand years. Here is his conclusion:

> Any human society is free to choose either to display great energy or to enjoy sexual freedom. The evidence is that they cannot do both for more than one generaion.[36]

We're dealing not only with sexual behavior that leads to spiritual death and in many instances to physical death, but we're also confronting the possible death of a culture. It's time we took a serious, thoughtful look at our sexual values.

RECOGNIZE SEDUCTION'S APPROACH

When cattle smell the slaughterhouse they start to bellow. When deer sense a noose they take to their heels. When birds spy out snares they spread their wings. But the young man in this story does nothing but go right ahead. Why? Because he doesn't understand seduction.

Seduction is nothing new; there's really no excuse for being suckered. Eve was seduced, of course, but it was all new to her. How exactly was she drawn in? Look at Genesis 3:1-7:

1. There was a subtle questioning of God's Word: "Did God really say . . . ?"
2. There was a blatant, exaggerated misrepresentation of what God had actually said: "You must not eat from *any* tree in the garden" (italics added).
3. There was an outright contradiction of what God had said: "You will not surely die."
4. There was a distorted representation of the character of God: "God knows it's really like this, but he's telling you differently."
5. There was a lying promise with an overwhelming offer: "You will be like God."

How can anyone guard against such crafty, outright seduction? It wouldn't be difficult to resist if its offers weren't so attractive. Present-day seduction to sexual immorality has a similar timbre:

"Has God really said that sex outside marriage is wrong?"

"God doesn't condemn sex outside of marriage if you really love each other."

"God knows your sexual needs. After all, he created them. He would want them to be satisfied."

"Don't worry. You will not be held accountable by God for your sex life. That's something that priests, puritans, and preachers have dreamed up because they're afraid that someone somewhere might be having some fun."

Derek Kidner's wise words are worth noting:

> God allowed the forbidden fruit its full appeal. The pattern of sin runs through the act, for Eve listened to a creature instead of the Creator, followed her impressions against her instructions, and made self-fulfillment her goal.[37]

We are confronted with the human contradiction of divine principle, to which we are tempted to respond on the basis of impressions rather than God's instructions. If our objective is not to please God but to please ourselves, we are at that moment vulnerable to seduction of all kinds, including sexual seduction. This is an area in which we can see the clear difference between deriving our values from ourselves, our society, or from a sovereign, all-knowing Lord.

RESIST SEDUCTION'S ATTACK

How do we resist when seduction slinks our way?

Above all else, guard your heart,
for it is the wellspring of life.

Put away perversity from your mouth;
keep corrupt talk far from your lips.
Let your eyes look straight ahead,
fix your gaze directly before you.
Make level paths for your feet
and take only ways that are firm.
Do not swerve to the right or the left;
keep your foot from evil.

PROVERBS 4:23-27

Let me summarize this passage in four basic principles:

- Guard your heart
- Clean up your conversation
- Focus your attention
- Watch your step

Guard Your Heart

We've already mentioned the crucial role the heart plays. If we are to guard the heart, from what are we to guard it? Among the seven things that God finds "detestable" is a heart that "devises wicked schemes" (Prov. 6.18). The woman in the story was obviously doing that, and the young man in all probability was doing likewise; why else would he have wandered down to her end of town? If both of them had been careful about the inner workings of their hearts, they would not have finished up where they did. Instead of guarding their hearts they were devising schemes that were immoral and destructive.

Sometime ago I was speaking at a pastors' conference. One of the other speakers gave a two-hour lecture entitled "How to Affair-Proof Your Marriage." That it was felt necessary to address this subject at a pastors' conference is surely a sobering commentary on the dilapidated state of some clergy values! I listened with great attention to the information shared with the pastors and then discussed it with a close friend, a psychologist. When I asked him what he thought about the intricate detail of the talk, he surprised me by saying, "There is no real need to go into all that detail. All men need to do is to be strictly honest with themselves. If they regularly check their thought life and are strictly honest about their motives, they will find their behavior appropriate." In other words, "Guard your heart." It is when the heart gives reign to "devise wicked schemes" that trouble brews.

So far, so good, but how are we to guard a heart that has such potential for devising wicked schemes? As we might expect, Proverbs has answers:

> *My son, keep your father's commands*
> *and do not forsake your mother's teaching.*
> *Bind them upon your heart forever;*
> *fasten them around your neck.*
> *When you walk, they will guide you;*
> *when you sleep, they will watch over you;*
> *when you awake, they will speak to you.*
> *For these commands are a lamp,*
> *this teaching is a light,*
> *and the corrections of discipline*
> *are the way to life,*
> *keeping you from the immoral woman,*
> *from the smooth tongue of the wayward wife.*
> *Do not lust in your heart after her beauty.*
> PROVERBS 6:20-25

The heart is capable of either lusting or listening. It can either allow itself to be captivated by that which seduces to evil, or it can be cultivated by the truth that leads to righteousness. It all depends on the degree of care given to guarding the heart against that which destroys and building it up with that which honors God.

When Paul was trying to help the Corinthian believers as they struggled with the sexual environment of their city, he had trenchant words to say that bear repeating in our not-so-dissimilar culture. Corinth was the "permissive society" before any such term was coined. One of their favorite proverbs was "Everything is permissible," which was a stupid thing to say. Paul's retort, "But not everything is beneficial," was right on target. The Corinthians also said, "Food for the stomach and the stomach for food," which seems harmless enough; but they went a step further and insisted in effect, "The body for sex and sex for the body." At that point Paul answered with, "The body is not meant for sexual immorality, but for the Lord, and the Lord for the body" (see 1 Cor. 6:13).

In other words, he was saying: You can make a logical argument that stomachs and food are made for each other. Stomachs can be regarded as very sophisticated gastronomical machines that process food, turn it into energy, and get rid of the waste. But you cannot project from that, however, that bodies and sex are made for each other, that bodies are sophisticated sex machines. Why? Because while stomachs are designed to process food, which passes away in a matter of hours, bodies are an integral part of a complete person—body, soul, mind, and spirit. Humans are made capable of fellowship with the divine to the remarkable extent of being indwelt by God's Spirit, and the body is part of that humanness. The body is much more than a sex machine. In fact, every part of a human being has a spiritual dimension, including the body—including sexuality! The whole person, including the body, is to be dedicated to the Lord so that the Lord can be dedicated to the body. The body is a temple of the Holy Spirit.

The body is not only infinitely more complex than a superb piece of physicality, but it is an integral part of a unique creation designed for divine habitation. Any argument that assumes that, in the same way that the body gets hungry and thirsty but is satisfied with food and water, so also it gets sexually aroused and should be satisfied with sex, is relegating the body to animal status. Instead, the body needs to be elevated to temple-of-the-Holy-God status.

But we also guard the heart by protecting it from illicit arousal, from being inflamed. "Do not lust in your heart after her beauty or let her captivate you" is a word for men living in a sex-saturated society. It is perfectly appropriate to recognize beauty. It's perfectly appropriate to appreciate beauty. It is utterly wrong to lust after beauty in the sense of generating such a fantasy desire for it that you wish to possess it.

It is impossible to escape completely from potentially arousing situations or potentially arousing people. Martin Luther made a good point when he said, "I can't stop birds from flying over my head, but I can stop them nesting in my hair." And that's the problem today—too many birds nesting where they don't belong. So we need to remember that there are positive and negative aspects to guarding our hearts. In the positive sense we bind truth upon it; in the negative sense we banish lust from it.

Clean up Your Conversation

One of the ways we clean up our conversation is by recognizing that there is a direct connection between lust in the heart and corrupt talk on the lips. They feed on each other. Conversation that is unguarded about sexual matters generates lust. Lust in the heart is often spewed out in language, and conversational topics today are full of sexual innuendo or worse. The Bible has a simple rule. It says that out of the abundance of the heart, the mouth speaks. That is why it is so sad to listen to some people speak. What comes out is a reflection of what's inside them. Have you ever noticed how much corrupt talk addresses such subjects as bodily functions, the opposite sex, and sexual activity—all in demeaning terms? You don't need to think of all the swear words you know, but most of them fit into that category. This is a reflection of commonly held perverted views of the body, sex, and sexuality.

Not only is the word coming out of the mouth a reflection of what's inside, but what comes out of the mouth can negatively affect what is inside. The more we find ourselves enjoying titillating conversation, the more likely our hearts are infected—which is dangerous in a seductive situation. That is why we need to heed the injunction, "Put away perversity from your mouth." That is why we must add "Clean up your conversation" to "Guard your heart."

Focus Your Attention

"Let your eyes look straight ahead, fix your gaze directly before you" (Prov. 4:25). In other words, focus your attention. Job did. He said, "I made a covenant with my eyes not to look lustfully at a girl" (Job 31:1). Too bad David didn't operate on that principle when he saw Bathsheba. Joseph was smarter than David when confronted with the aggressive and available Mrs. Potiphar. He didn't want to focus on what she had to offer; he was more interested in what he was going to do with his life, and he had no time for diversions that were contrary to his divinely ordained goals.

I have often been impressed by the remarkable concentration of big-time athletes. They seem to block out the crowd, the noise, and all other distractions and to concentrate on the game with fierce intensity—"Keep your eye on the ball." They know that the shortest lapse in concentration can result in an error, a fumble, a lost game, even a lost championship.

We need the same kind of keen concentration if we are to maintain our sexual integrity. Our sexuality is so much a part of who we are as persons, and yet it is so easily warped and damaged when we lose our vision of who we are in the divine plan. We are unique creatures of so much worth that God made a way to be eternally connected to us—at great cost to himself. We have the capacity to enjoy the very life of God inside us, to be empowered by the Holy Spirit day by day, yet we so easily relinquish the honor and health of our bodies, even though they are the temples in which God dwells here on earth.

Sex can become all-consuming; it can cause us to wander off the path of our careers, our marriages, and our ministries. Rather than develop the many wonderful gifts of personality and spirit that are waiting to shine through our lives, we squander our energies on immediate physical gratification. We need the concentration of a winning athlete, the dedication of a person who knows where he or she is going in life. That's why I am so encouraged by the David Robinsons and A. C. Greens of this world. Our sexuality is meant to enhance our lives, not consume them.

Watch Your Step

Proverbs exhorts us to "take only ways that are firm"—to watch our steps (4:26). Now, all this sounds like a lot of rules and regulations. But we must remember that when we come to God in repentance and seek his forgiveness for all manner of sin, including sexual sin, he forgives us for Christ's sake, and he gives us his Spirit. With the life of his Spirit growing in us, we find that our desires will change, and the right decisions will more often seem and feel right to us because our view of life is being transformed. There will always be temptation, but when we begin to experience how rich life can be when lived rightly and purely, our incentive to stay on those "firm ways" will grow.

For now, the rules help us keep to the way that is best for all concerned. Over time, God's law of love will be written in our hearts, and we will feel less and less that external laws are being imposed upon us. Our own desires will equate more and more with what God has been saying and desiring all along. And this, frankly, is what is needed in our society today if people are to live rightly before God in the area of their sexuality. Mere rule keeping will not change the course of society, although it can certainly grant some protection. But true transformation within us, as we discover the high quality our lives can have before a loving God, should be our constant aim.

SEXUAL DELIGHT

Proverbs is not at all prudish about sexuality. While illicit sex is roundly condemned, the full enjoyment of sexual delight in the context of marriage is unabashedly commended. This should not surprise us, since God invented sex in the first place. Unfortunately, we have to give so much energy to exposing the abuses of this beautiful gift that it is easy for the untaught to gain the impression that sex, of itself, is bad and that God is against it. But we can let go of our hesitancy by meditating on the following.

> *Drink water from your own cistern,*
> *running water from your own well.*
> *Should your springs overflow in the streets,*
> *your streams of water in the public squares?*
> *Let them be yours alone,*
> *never to be shared with strangers.*
> *May your fountain be blessed,*
> *and may you rejoice in the wife of your youth.*
> *A loving doe, a graceful deer—*
> *may her breasts satisfy you always,*
> *may you ever be captivated by her love.*
>
> PROVERBS 5:15-19

Even the most unpoetic among us can understand that! And it sounds good because it is good.

What does a man get for all the toil and anxious striving with which
he labors under the sun? All his days his work is pain and grief;
even at night his mind does not rest. This too is meaningless.
KING SOLOMON, ECCLESIASTES 2:22-23

Whatever you do, whether in word or deed, do it all in the name of the Lord Jesus.
THE APOSTLE PAUL, COLOSSIANS 3:17

A couple of men were working one day. One man was digging a hole and the other man was watching him dig. As
soon as the hole was completed, the second man sprang into action
and filled it in! A person who was observing said to them, "That's a
very peculiar job you're doing. Why do you dig the hole and then fill
it in?" The workmen replied, "Well, usually there are three men on
this team. The first one digs the hole, the second one plants a tree and
the third one fills it in. But the second guy went deer hunting."

WORK AS A REASON FOR EXISTING

There are those for whom work has become the be-all and end-all of
their existence. Only in their work do they find meaning. Only in the
things that their work provides do they discover personal significance. For them work is not an act of worship unto the Lord. Rather,
work is what they worship, and the products of that work are the idols
before which they bow. They are not working out of any sense of

being created in the divine image or of producing something that will glorify God and benefit the community. They're working because work is their only reason for being, and the money their work provides gives them the things that they crave—the symbols of prestige, the status, the preferential treatment, the shortcuts to where they want to go, the shields against life's unpleasantness—the "best" of everything. It is purely self-oriented, and it often leads them to neglect spouse and family and leisure and worship and voluntary service. Relationships founder, and health is jeopardized.

WORK AS AN IMPOSITION TO BE BORNE

Some people perceive work as an imposition to be borne. Their attitude is truculent and uncooperative, and their approach is not even close to an "honest day's work for an honest day's pay." It is usually characterized by intense dislike of management on one hand and intense distrust of labor on the other. Bitterness, lack of direction, and laziness are all too apparent when we discuss the workplace with many people today.

Managers tell me of employees calling in sick when they are well, taking home what they believe is theirs when it clearly isn't, arriving late, skipping out early—generally ripping off the company wherever they can because they are convinced that they are being ripped off. No wonder there's bitterness! One company went so far as to post this announcement on its bulletin board:

> Sometime between starting and quitting time, without infringing on lunch periods, coffee breaks, rest periods, storytelling, ticket selling, holiday planning, and the rehashing of yesterday's television programs, we ask that each employee try to find some time for a work break. This may seem radical, but it might aid steady employment and assure regular paychecks.

But not all the blame rests with the employees. I have a friend, a business executive, who has been "let go" three times from three different companies in the space of a few years. Another friend went in for an interview at which he expected to be honored because he had produced more business than any other man in the company. Instead he was told to clear out his desk by noon. He had been replaced by a younger man who could do the job for considerably less pay. In a pastors' conference a number of years ago, I was informed that approximately half of the attendees had been fired by their churches at one time or another, with no recourse and less warning.

THE MEANINGLESSNESS OF WORK

But many people have a terrible sense of meaninglessness and aimlessness in the workplace. Their work is mundane, repetitive, mind-numbing, cog-in-a-machine, no-sense-of-end-product labor. They are frustrated, watching-the-clock, "can't wait for Friday" people. And it shows! Daniel Yankelovich, in his book *New Rules*, reported on research done in one of America's motor industry giants:

> Symptoms of worker frustration were visible
> everywhere . . . in absenteeism, tardiness, carelessness,
> indifference, high turnover, the number of union
> grievances, slowdowns in the periods preceding
> collective bargaining, and even sabotage. But mostly,
> worker frustration was seen in poor product quality.[38]

Twenty-seven percent of workers in that particular factory said that under no circumstances would they ever buy the products that they were making themselves.

According to Scripture, one of the main problems with human beings at work is laziness. After extolling the industry of the ant, Proverbs goes on to expose the indolence of the sluggard. We don't hear the term *sluggard* much anymore, but it sounds just like some folks.

How long will you lie there, you sluggard?
When will you get up from your sleep?
A little sleep, a little slumber,
a little folding of the hands to rest—
and poverty will come on you like a bandit
and scarcity like an armed man.

PROVERBS 6:9-11

The sluggard is not painted in very glowing terms here! But there's more:

The sluggard says, "There is a lion in the road,
a fierce lion roaming the streets!"
As a door turns on its hinges,
so a sluggard turns on his bed.
The sluggard buries his hand in the dish;
he is too lazy to bring it back to his mouth.
The sluggard is wiser in his own eyes
than seven men who answer discreetly.

PROVERBS 26:13-16

Here is somebody who is committed to procrastination, somebody who worships relaxation, who is an expert at rationalization, and who utterly lacks motivation. A sluggard has little sense of what it really means to be a human being created in the divine image, possessing latent abilities for creativity and productivity with which to glorify God and contribute to society.

FROM SUNDAY TO MONDAY

It's common to find people who believe in certain spiritual values but keep them in watertight compartments and do not allow them to impinge upon their daily lives. That is the kind of lifestyle that segregates Sunday in church from Monday in the office! But this is not the way spirituality was meant to be! True spirituality enters every area of life, giving it newness, energy, and clarity. As we have seen in the book of Proverbs, values stemming from God's character and his purposes for us will affect the decisions we make relating to our marriages, the way we bring up our children, and our sexual behavior. These values should also revolutionize the way we see work and approach it.

When we consider that approximately half our waking hours are spent working, it's in our best interest to discover what work is supposed to mean to us! And if we don't have the right understanding of and approach to work, something is sadly out of sync with us during 50 percent of our lives. That should give pause for thought to any living, breathing human being.

A CAREFUL LOOK AT ANTS

It may not have occurred to many of us that the ant is a superb role model for modern people! But since Scripture says that it is, we should at least look into this curious example God has given us.

Go to the ant, you sluggard;
consider its ways and be wise!
It has no commander,
no overseer or ruler,
yet it stores its provisions in summer
and gathers its food at harvest.

PROVERBS 6:6-8

Sometime when you are out in the woods, lift up a rock and take a look. Chances are, there's life under there. Ant life. The reaction of a community of ants when exposed to sudden discovery will provide food for thought. As you watch them scurry, you will see that there is method to their scurrying. They are remarkably industrious and organized. They can have all their eggs and other belongings, whatever they are, moved out of sight into underground tunnels in a matter of minutes. As ants and bees are related it is not surprising to find that ants are, if you'll pardon the expression, as busy as bees.

These insects live tragically brief lives (unless they sting or bite you, and then we think they have lived far too long!), but during their short sojourn they appear to have clearly defined tasks for which they are ideally suited. Sometimes just for a day! Next day they've changed, they have different abilities, they're given an entirely different task. But they know what they're doing, they know what they're capable of, they know what they're gifted for, they have an understanding of purpose and objective, and they work hard. Then they're dead!

GOD WORKS

Fortunately the behavior of the ant is not the only model of the workplace available to us. Right at the beginning of Scripture we are introduced to God without preamble. "In the beginning God. . . ." And what is he doing? He's working! For six intense "days" he works, but "by the seventh day God had finished the work he had being doing" (Gen. 2:2).

Now the idea that God goes to work may be a novel thought for some! But he does and the fact that he does shows that there is something intrinsically right about work. Not only that, but when God examined what he had produced through work, he pronounced it good. We can reasonably assume, therefore, that work is fundamentally right and good and, accordingly, is the right and good thing for us to be doing. And, like God, we may be thoroughly justified in being pleased with the results of our work—provided that we have been doing the right thing and that we have done a good job!

PEOPLE WORK

Part of what God worked to produce was us! And what did he do with the first human beings? He put them in Paradise.

Paradise! What images that word conjures up for us: Tahiti, where soft breezes lazily stir the thick, green fronds of stately palms, while turquoise breakers roll on white sandy beaches at the feet of dusky maidens bearing cool drinks, which we sip languorously until we drift into relaxing sleep. That, I suppose, is the travel-guide image of Paradise—of Eden. But the experience of the original occupants of Paradise was somewhat different. God put them in Paradise and he put them to work! They were put in charge of that vast garden and were commissioned to be keepers of the other creatures who lived in it. They were created to do something—not to lie on a beach. To be a human is to be a worker.

But things went wrong. Human beings rebelled against God, and as a result, their relationship with God, with each other, and with their environment fragmented and fractured. We call this event the Fall. One of the consequences of the Fall, according to Scripture, was that work would be shot through with toil and tedium. In graphic terms God explained to the chagrined couple, "Cursed is the ground because of you; through painful toil you will eat of it. . . . by the sweat of your brow you will eat your food" (Gen. 3:17-19). So when modern people find work toilsome and tedious, they're not experiencing work as it was intended to be. They're experiencing the consequences of the Fall. The negative aspects of work with which we are so often familiar were completely lacking when life began as God intended.

Try this little exercise. Imagine doing something you really enjoy doing. Maybe you're good at crafts, writing, organizing events, talking with people, programming computers, fixing things, or inventing and designing. Imagine doing what you enjoy doing and what you're good at doing—without any backaches, headaches, weeds among the plants, troublemakers among the people, viruses on your computer, and so on. The work goes well, the results are fabulous, the feelings of accomplishment are deep and lasting and everybody is delighted with all that you have done. Your energy knows no bounds, your enthusiasm no limits. Perhaps you can remember an occasional day like that. It was a taste of God's original intent for our activity on earth. Only after mankind sinned and was cast from the garden did the weeds grow and human conflict spoil it all. Originally work was a delight.

JESUS WORKED

The good news, of course, is that Jesus came into the world to roll back the consequences of the Fall. For thirty years he worked his way through life as a craftsman, then laid aside that occupation and committed himself to a specific ministry. When he was baptized—at the conclusion of his thirty years of manual labor—the Father said he was well pleased! And at the end of his public ministry Jesus told his Father that he had finished "the work you gave me to do" (John 17:4). As Jesus stood on the Mount of Transfiguration near the end of his public ministry, his Father again stated his warm approval of the work Jesus had done. Jesus was no stranger to work, whether the dirt-under-the-nails work of a village carpentry shop or the life-draining work of giving fallen people new life. The way he worked met with the Father's full approval.

WHAT CAN WORK MEAN TO US NOW?

If the work of redemption rolls back the consequences of the Fall, then redeemed people may experience a totally new approach to work. They will begin to see work as something that they were created and redeemed to do, and they will embark upon it with delight and great enthusiasm. All this is foundational to our understanding of work, and should provide the basis of our work ethic.

Human beings were made in the "image of God."

The highly significant phrase, "image of God," has been interpreted in a variety of ways. But this statement, taken from Genesis chapter 1, appears in the context of God being creative and productive. Those who were made in the image of God at the very time he was in the act of producing them would themselves demonstrate the divine image through creative and productive lives. There's a very real sense in which human beings are uniquely creative and uniquely productive. Beavers build dams, and birds build nests, but human beings are obviously in a class of their own. If this is true, then the more creative and productive I am, the more likely I am to be fulfilling the uniqueness of my humanity.

Having designated humanity's unique status, God then said that we should exercise dominion over his creation. We were given the responsibility and the ability to move around in the divine creation, to discover its wonders, and to put them to use for the glory of God and for the benefit of humanity. This is something, of course, from which we benefit every moment of our lives.

These words were spoken to perfect human beings living in an ideal world. Since we know very little about Paradise and human activity at the beginning of time, we can only speculate on what this mandate for dominion involved. But we don't need to speculate on what it means in a fallen universe. When the Indians roamed Manhattan, hunting and fishing and living off the land, there was not a lot there. No doubt it was smog free, pristine, and lovely. But human ingenuity, creativity, hard work, and brilliant utilization of the raw materials God had placed at human disposal produced the magnificent buildings and towering skyscrapers of modern New York. Hospitals and universities, art galleries and churches, airports and sea terminals, Wall Street and the United Nations, and a thousand other edifices stand in tall testimony to mankind's fulfillment of the divine mandate to work and to utilize divinely granted resources.

But on September 11, 2001, a group of human beings showed their evil genius by flying passenger airliners into the twin towers of the World Trade Center in New York City, killing thousands of unsuspecting people. It was a series of acts of unprecedented horror and devastation. Humankind has the capacity for mighty acts of creativity, but because of the Fall it also has vast potential for unmitigated evil. We are perversely capable of mighty works of blessing or cursing, of productiveness or destructiveness.

Jesus came into the world, not to be served, but to serve.
Jesus had a keen appreciation of human need and he was absolutely committed to applying himself to meeting that need. He insisted that he had not come to be served but rather to serve. He instructed his disciples to emulate his example and to foster his attitude—the servant spirit.

When we adopt a servant spirit and channel it into meeting the needs of the world around us, we will work. When we think in these terms, it's easy to see how a servant attitude in the workplace, home, or church that translates into productive, helpful activity will be a mirror of discipleship. Following Jesus means, among other things, doing what he did. Followers of Jesus will be servants, and servanthood involves work.

When people observe the way Jesus' disciples live, they should "see their good works and glorify their Father who is in heaven."
The work of Jesus' disciples should bear testimony about their faith. If you see workers who are aimless on the job, who are careless about their work, and who regard their work as utterly meaningless, you have discovered people who don't have much of a theology of work. They are bearing testimony that their attitudes toward the workplace are not from God himself. On the other hand, if you find people who demonstrate in their work habits that they belong to God, you will see the difference in attitude and productivity, and you will recognize and applaud it.

God has called us to be coworkers with him.
God put people in Eden, in the first place, in order to manage his creation for him. The apostle Paul stated specifically that we are co-

workers together with God. There are some professions in which it is easier than others to see how we are coworkers with God in fulfilling his purposes, but if we are doing what we believe God wants us to be doing, then we are working with him in accomplishing his purposes.

I like the story of the pastor who was visiting one of his church members who happened to be a farmer. After walking around the farm, they took a coffee break. Sitting on the porch looking over the ordered fields, the pastor, waxing spiritual, said, "Isn't it wonderful to see what God has done with his creation?" To this the old farmer said, "Sure is, and you should've seen what a mess it was when he had it on his own." This is actually quite correct from a theological standpoint. There is a sense in which God's creation is a bit of a mess on its own. But when man comes along as the divinely ordained coworker, it's amazing what can be done. What a wonderful thing it is to go to work knowing that you are cooperating with God in bringing his purposes to fruition!

Our ultimate motivation should be to glorify God in all that we do.
Some people work to please the boss; some people work simply to put in the time; some people work in order to get a paycheck; some people work because they just have to work. Often tedium and toil go to work with them each day.

Other people work because they believe that in exercising their abilities, channeling their energies, and utilizing their time, they are actually glorifying God. They know that they did not create their skills, time, or energy. These are God's gifts, and when they exercise them in appropriate endeavors, they glorify God. And when we channel our resources into creative, productive activity that contributes to the community's well-being, we have crowned our work with true glory from heaven.

In the sixth century A.D., St. Benedict of Nursia wrote his Benedictine

Rule as a guide for the communal life of the monastery at Monte Cassino, Italy. His Rule contained a prologue and seventy-three chapters and covered every aspect of life in the monastery. But in time the community adopted as its motto, *Orare est laborare; laborare est orare*, which means, "To pray is to work; to work is to pray ." Many people assume that the occupants of a monastery's austere buildings spend all their time praying, singing, and confessing their sins. But that is certainly not what Benedict had in mind. He looked for monks who were deeply committed to prayer and equally committed to work. In fact, they were taught not to differentiate between the two. When they worked, it was an act of prayer; when they prayed, they worked at it with all their hearts.

Nicholas Herman was a "great awkward fellow who broke everything." After serving as a soldier and working as a footman, he entered the Carmelite Order at fifty years of age. He was assigned to the kitchen and he was not happy about the posting. But he learned to wash dishes as an act of love for the Lord. As a result, at the kitchen sink he began to discover the presence of God. After he died, his writings on the theme of God's presence were published in a book entitled *The Practice of the Presence of God,* under the name of Brother Lawrence. To this day, four centuries later, his book still captures the hearts and minds of its readers. For him, washing dishes was an expression of love for the Lord—it was worship disguised as work.

My mother was a very godly and very disciplined lady. She tried to instill her values into me when I was a teenager. Every night before bedtime I was required to clean everybody's shoes. Often after I had finished cleaning them she would say, "That's not good enough," and she would proceed to clean them all over again. Then she would hand them back to me and say, "You clean shoes as if they belonged to the Lord Jesus—and you clean them as if they would be worn by him."

If believers went to work on Monday morning with this attitude, not griping like everybody else or simply discussing Sunday football, but applying themselves to work as if it were an act of worship, they, along with their work and the workplace environment, would change dramatically for the better.

Just think of what it would be like in a car pool on Monday morning if the driver greeted everybody with "Good morning—here we go to worship." The travelers might even prepare themselves by praying about the activities of the day, interceding on behalf of their workmates, and laying before the Lord the decisions they would be faced with and the problems they would confront. Then they would be close to fulfilling Paul's injunction: "Whatever you do, whether in word or deed, do it all in the name of the Lord Jesus" (Col. 3:17).

When we work, we function as providers.
Paul told the Thessalonians, "When we were with you, we gave you this rule: 'If a man will not work, he shall not eat'" (2 Thess. 3:10). No ambiguity there. It does not say, however, that if a man *cannot* work he shall not eat. And it doesn't say that if a man cannot *find* work, he shall not eat. Some people have been very harsh at this point, not understanding the problems of the unemployed or the handicapped. But those who have the ability and opportunity to work and *will* not work are failing to do what they were created to do. Human beings are designed to work in order to provide for their own needs.

And not only for their own needs. The Bible also says, "If anyone does not provide for his relatives, and especially for his immediate family, he has denied the faith and is worse than an unbeliever" (1 Tim. 5:8). That's tough talk by any standard, but it doesn't end there. The Ephesian believers were instructed: "He who has been stealing must steal no longer, but must work, doing something useful with his own hands, that he may have something to share with those in need" (Eph. 4:28). The thief must be rehabilitated; he must become self-supporting by honest means, and he must produce a surplus in order that he may provide for the needy. If that is true of reformed thieves, it surely applies to the rest of us. We work not only to support ourselves and those who are dependent upon us, but we work in order to produce value that can then be transferred to people who are in need.

We also work in order to finance the work of the Lord. Now, I'm not going to belabor this point. When we offer to the Lord the financial results of our work, as an act of worship, that is an act of great value. The offering then finances the work of the Lord and brings blessing to other people's lives. What a privilege to be able to work at a bench in order to produce value, which in turn becomes an offering in worship, which then brings eternal blessing to someone I will never meet on the other side of the world! Billy Graham used to say, "I can't understand how a brown cow eating green grass can give white milk and yellow butter—but I believe it!" Here's something else that is true, but hard to believe: Forty hours of digging ditches produces value. When it is placed in an offering plate in a church, it becomes an act of worship. Then it finds its way across the seas to a tiny woman living in a squatter camp in Cambodia, making it possible for her to have a roof over her head, food in her stomach, Christ in her heart, and a church in her shack. Tell me that isn't hard to believe! But it's true, and it works when we understand the profound significance of work.

THE DIFFERENCE BETWEEN WORK AND EMPLOYMENT

Today we find many people who are not working, not because they don't want to, but because there is no work available to them. They are eager to work, but employment opportunities aren't there. It's very easy for them to become discouraged, feeling that they lack significance and that their humanity is being depreciated.

Let me differentiate here between work and employment. I believe that when there is no employment—that is, work for remuneration—available to us, that does not mean that we cannot work. We should encourage those who are unemployed to find, either inside or outside the community of believers, opportunities to do something creative, productive, and significant, even though they may not receive pay for it. Being unemployed does not mean that a person cannot give an offering to God, care for the family, or help those in need; it merely means that the recompense for these activities may not be money. We can still give gifts of our time, talent, and energy.

Retired people should never get the idea that God created them to work till their late fifties or early sixties and then quit. That was never the divine intention. If they are fortunate enough to be in a position to retire, wonderful. This means that they can channel their creativity and the wisdom they've accumulated over the years into new ventures, new personal goals, and new areas of ministry. Retirement should never mean that people stop being creative and productive or that they cease to invest their lives for God's glory and channel their energies to the benefit of the community. What it can mean is that they have more time to do it, and they can do it on a volunteer basis.

When the time comes that there is no need to maintain civilization and there are no more human needs to meet, work might then be unnecessary. Until that day, however, work is in order, and workers are needed. Paradise is not a vacation—it is a vocation.

Money ranks with love as man's greatest joy.
And it ranks with death as his greatest source of anxiety.
JOHN KENNETH GALBRAITH

*M*oney talks, loud and clear, and what it says is not always pretty.

Take the responses of ordinary Americans to the question, "What
would you do for $10 million?"[39]

25 percent would leave their families.

25 percent would leave their church and/or religion.

23 percent said they would be a prostitute for a week or more.

7 percent were willing to kill a stranger for that kind of money.

Apparently decisions can be prompted by monetary gain. Values are
for sale.

After the survey was taken, the researchers wondered if the $10
million tab had been too tempting. So they asked the same people,
"What would you do for $5 million, for $4 million, for $3 million?"
The responses were the same. The good news is that at $2 million
people began to have second thoughts.

The way we look at money affects our view of life in general. The
value we place on finances can very often be the most dominant of all

our values. The lure of money can take the most crucial place in our decision making process. Paul expressed real insight when he told Timothy, "The love of money is a root of all kinds of evil" (1 Tim. 6:10). Paul did not say, as he is so often misquoted, "Money is the root of all evil." It's the love of it, not the presence of it, that is so dangerous. Much evil flows from an inordinate love of money.

Where do we need to start in our desire to make right decisions in the handling of our finances? Let's look at Proverbs once again.

In all your ways acknowledge him,
and he will make your paths straight.

PROVERBS 3:6

"In all your ways" could not be more inclusive! In all aspects of life we are to acknowledge the Lord, and he will act on our behalf. He will make our paths straight. This does not mean that there will be no potholes or roadblocks, but it does mean there will be a clear sense of direction from above in those areas we commit to God.

Money is a very sensitive subject. We tend to be protective of our resources and defensive when questioned about them. So we might be tempted to interpret "in all your ways" as "in all your ways except your finances"! Yet this passage of Scripture goes on to say with inescapable clarity:

Honor the LORD with your wealth,
with the firstfruits of all your crops;
then your barns will be filled to overflowing,
and your vats will brim over with new wine.

PROVERBS 3:9-10

We shouldn't hesitate to see ourselves in these verses just because they use the word "wealth." Most of us probably don't consider ourselves wealthy. It's the guy who has a bigger house, drives a better car, and takes more dramatic vacations who is wealthy! So we don't regard wealth—or proverbs about wealth—as relevant. The guy next door is the one who needs to read these proverbs!

However, when compared to the majority of people in our world, any person who can afford to buy this book is wealthy. In fact, compared with people in Indonesia, Laos, Cambodia, and Vietnam, all of which I have visited in recent years, we are fabulously wealthy. So let's not assume that because somebody next door drives a shiny Mercedes and we drive a rusty Pinto, this talk of wealth is not for us. But let's not be distracted from the main point of these proverbs: We must honor the Lord with our possessions, however vast or meager.

The Lord was promising his covenant people that the path to general well-being starts with acknowledging him, with honoring him. The Hebrew words used in these verses mean "to worship" or "to esteem greatly." God's people were to put the Lord first in everything, including the way they handled their wealth.

I believe that the Lord has given us principles concerning our finances—whether we have much or little, own land or rent an apartment, are direct descendants of the Hebrews or are not even sure who our ancestors are. The Lord knows that money has the power to enrich our lives or destroy them completely. He has given us guidelines that not only honor him but protect us.

RICH AND POOR HAVE SOMETHING IN COMMON

While it is obvious that the circumstances of the ancient covenant people living in the Promised Land were quite different from the situations in which we live today, there are similarities that we must not overlook.

Rich and poor have this in common:
The LORD is the Maker of them all.
PROVERBS 22:2

I am writing this chapter sitting on the balcony of a twelfth-floor apartment in Caracas, Venezuela. Far below me are well-groomed gardens, shady jogging trails, and inviting swimming pools surrounded by multicolored umbrellas. All around me rooftops are festooned with satellite dishes that reach to the heavens to bring in television programs from around the world. Winding roads are blocked by expensive automobiles. Meanwhile, just across the bustling freeway, perched precariously on steep hillsides, are teeming shantytowns where thousands scratch and scrape for survival, where disease is chronic, and where crime is ever present. Here, the rich and the poor live within yards of each other—yet they are miles apart.

But these words from Proverbs remind us that people living in entirely different worlds still have the same Maker; they all are created by and for him.

IT'S MY MONEY

Let's take this a step further. You've no doubt heard people exclaim, "It's my money!" Is that strictly true? That is, is it the whole truth? When Israel entered the Land of Promise, if they became prosperous they might be tempted to insist that "It's my money!" So the Lord reminded them, "Remember the LORD your God, for it is he who gives you the ability to produce wealth" (Deut. 8:18). Most people are flabbergasted when they hear this statement for the first time. The people of Israel were no exception! They were just as likely to proclaim, "My power and the strength of my hands have produced this wealth for me" (Deut. 8:17). This very attitude prompted the Lord to remind them that without him, there would be no wealth and there would be no work. In fact, there would be no "them"! Paul hit the same note when he asked the Corinthians, "What do you have that you did not receive?" (1 Cor. 4:7). The answer, of course, is "Nothing."

God gives men and women the power to produce wealth, and wealth is related to productive activity, so ultimately we owe our wealth to the God who gave us the ability, energy, means, and skill to produce our "market value." We can hone our skills, but we can't create them out of nothing. We can use or abuse time, but we can't even stretch it, let alone make more of it. We can place food in our mouths, but we can't create from it the energy that will stimulate a brain cell, trigger a memory, communicate a concept, or flex a muscle. Skills, time, and energy are gifts. We, both rich and poor, are dependent on our Maker for all that it takes to produce wealth. Wriggle as we might, there is no getting away from it: "It is he who gives you the ability to produce wealth."

Labor—the expenditure of skills, time, and energy—is the means whereby we produce value in the form of goods and services. That value is usually measured in terms of money. So,

The exercise of God-given skills, time, and energy = *labor*.
Labor produces goods and services, which have *value*.
Value is transferred using *money*.
Money is therefore an extension of a *person*.

How then are we to honor the Lord with our wealth? One of the most obvious ways of doing it is in presenting the money as a worship offering. Since our wealth is an extension of our being, God accepts it as an offering of ourselves.

Richard J. Foster has pointed out:

Money has many characteristics of deity. It gives us security, can induce guilt, gives us freedom, gives us power, and seems to be omnipresent. Most sinister of all, however, is its bid for omnipotence.[40]

If money isn't handled very carefully and wisely, it will establish its reign in our lives. Jesus said, "Where your treasure is, there your heart will be also" (Luke 12:34), and, "You cannot serve both God and Money" (Matt. 6:24).

How do we guard against money becoming our god? We earn our money by gainful labor, we need our money to pay our bills, and the government wants our money to pay for their programs. In fact, money is a major, unavoidable, and indispensable part of our lives. How can we avoid it becoming all-important when it is so important? The answer is found in the admonition to "honor the Lord with our wealth." Our finances come under the Lord's direction, so we must handle our money according to his instructions. This will ensure that our wealth does not become our lord.

How Should We Accumulate Wealth?

> *Two things I ask of you, O LORD;*
> *do not refuse me before I die:*
> *Keep falsehood and lies far from me;*
> *give me neither poverty nor riches,*
> *but give me only my daily bread.*
> *Otherwise, I may have too much and disown you*
> *and say, "Who is the LORD?"*
> *Or I may become poor and steal,*
> *and so dishonor the name of my God.*
>
> PROVERBS 30:7-9

This is an incredibly mature attitude. It recognizes the temptations that either a shortage or an excess of money can bring. It sees honoring the Lord as more significant than making money. It admits to inherent weaknesses of character that need to be disciplined. It testifies to a willingness to be content with life's basics rather than chasing after life's luxuries.

John D. Rockefeller, the multimillionaire, was at least honest when asked, "How much money does it take to make a man happy?"

His reply: "Just a little more." Most people are critical of this kind of attitude, which shows itself when professional ball players, who earn enormous salaries for playing a boy's game, go on strike for more. Or when CEOs of Fortune 500 companies pull down vast salaries and huge stock options while factory workers in their companies are being laid off and losing their life savings. But given the chance to get "just a little more," how many of the critics would act any differently? I came across this anonymous poem some time ago:

> *Dug from the mountainside*
> *Or washing in the glen,*
> *Servant am I or master of men.*
> *Earn me, I bless you,*
> *Steal me, I curse you;*
> *Grasp me and hold me*
> *A fiend will possess you.*
> *Lie for me, die for me,*
> *Covet me, take me—*
> *Angel or devil*
> *I'm just what you make me.*

Money or wealth can be that which we possess or that which possesses us. If it's the former, it will be a means of blessing. If it's the latter, our love for it becomes a root of all kinds of evil.

BEING CONTENT WITH YOUR WAGES

"What should we do?" asked some soldiers. John replied, "Don't extort money, and don't accuse people of things you know they didn't do. And be content with your pay." LUKE 3:14 NLT

Recently, a number of Green Bay Packers intentionally took pay cuts to stay on the team and passed up chances of bigger paychecks with other teams. Granted, the Packers were winning at the time, and none of the players were heading for the poor house. But at least money was not the only driving force of their decision. It does happen!

Understanding the significance of work, we can go about our daily tasks, not with a view toward making a bundle, but with the intention of working well and accepting what we receive for it as from the Lord. This does not mean we eschew labor negotiations or refuse to talk with prospective employers about reasonable remuneration, but it does mean that making money is not the only driving force of our lives.

"There's Danger in Them There Bills"

The wealth of the rich is their fortified city;
they imagine it an unscalable wall.

PROVERBS 18:11

As I look out from my temporary office on this Caracas balcony, I can see apartment blocks with security guards, ornately barred windows, and double- and triple-locked doors. Every few minutes I hear alarms pierce the air as owners open their car doors and hurriedly unlock their safety devices and disconnect their electronic watchdogs. All in the name of security—and none of it comes cheaply!

On the other side of the freeway the people in the barrios have no such luxury; their meager possessions have no such security. Their precarious homes, far from looking like fortresses, give the impression that the next torrential downpour might wash them away. Money buys security. That's the upside. The downside? If money protects you, then the Lord is not necessary. It is no coincidence that there are far more believers in the barrios of the world than in the upscale neighborhoods. Paul was straightforward on this subject when he instructed Timothy:

> Command those who are rich in this present world not
> to be arrogant nor to put their hope in wealth, which is

152

so uncertain, but to put their hope in God, who richly
provides us with everything for our enjoyment.

1 TIMOTHY 6:17

This does not mean that if you can afford it and need it, a Doberman
might not be a good investment or an alarm system might not help
you sleep better. But in the end, it is the Lord who makes us secure.
Even the most elaborate precautions money can buy will make no
one immune to life's vicissitudes, and even the most expensive investment in personal protection cannot pay dividends of immortality. As
Paul said, wealth is very uncertain, and it has a tendency to erode our
spirituality. Wealth tends to seduce us into trusting it rather than
God.

Wealth also has the ability to desensitize those who pursue its accumulation. Let's face it—some people make money at other people's expense. One man's profit is another man's loss. The rich get
richer as the poor get poorer. This may be unavoidable to a certain extent, but there's no denying the attitude of insensitivity to others that
so often accompanies the accumulation of wealth.

He who oppresses the poor to increase his wealth
and he who gives gifts to the rich—both come to poverty.
PROVERBS 22:16

Not everybody is as crass as Marie Antoinette, who, on hearing that
the people were out of bread, said, "Let them eat cake." But an impoverished spirit and lack of compassion can overtake one's heart
when accumulating wealth becomes a main goal. Wealth can cause a
hardening of compassion's arteries.

John D. Rockefeller still wanted more, even though he would
have had a hard time spending all his money if he'd wanted to.
Money can do that to you. It can create an appetite that resists satisfaction. It wants more—more ease, more security, more peace of
mind, more prestige, more perks, more status symbols, more toys,

more trophies, more of whatever else money can buy. We have to exercise great care to ensure that the pursuit of wealth does not become an all-consuming passion that leaves us spiritually broke, emotionally drained, and relationally bereft. More than one man in his single-minded ambition to climb the corporate ladder has done so rung by rung, only to discover at the top rung that the ladder was leaning against the wrong building. En route he traded his wife, children, health, and friends, and he finished with a sense of loss—an impoverished soul.

Such people would do well to heed Proverbs before it is too late:

> *Do not wear yourself out to get rich;*
> *have the wisdom to show restraint.*
> *Cast but a glance at riches, and they are gone,*
> *for they will surely sprout wings*
> *and fly off to the sky like an eagle.*
>
> PROVERBS 23:4-5

Putting it another way:

> *That money talks*
> *I'll not deny.*
> *I heard it once.*
> *It said, "Good-bye."*

Wealth can erode restraint and common sense. Its accumulation can also erode principle. Vince Lombardi reputedly taught the Green Bay Packers, "Winning isn't everything—it's the only thing." We have to be concerned at such an approach. If winning is the only thing that matters, then any means of winning justifies this solitary end. Likewise, if making money is the only thing that matters, then principles may fly out the window. Honesty and integrity may be absorbed into "creative bookkeeping"; compassion for struggling competitors may get lost in "dog-eat-dog" philosophy; and shady practice may be excused because "it's a rat race out there." Maybe so—but not everybody has to become a rat.

The ancient book reminds us:

> *One eager to get rich will not go unpunished.*
>
> PROVERBS 28:20

We can honor the Lord with our wealth in the way that we accumulate it. There are right and wrong ways of doing it. The right ways honor God; the wrong ways are destructive to us.

MANAGE YOUR MONEY OR IT WILL MANAGE YOU

We can also honor the Lord in the way we administer our wealth—however much or little we may have accumulated. There are three main considerations: (1) establishing sound principles, (2) maintaining healthy perspectives, and (3) developing appropriate procedures.

1. Establishing sound principles.

Dos and don'ts don't sit well with most people. But we need them anyway. A former youth pastor, when talking to teenagers about sex, would give them the rules: Don't lie down. Don't take anything off. Don't touch below the neck. Not a do in sight—but three very good don'ts. They seemed to serve very well for the traumatic teenage years of raging hormones and confusing signals. He was kind enough, however, to send one of his former students a cable on his wedding day that said simply, "All three rules canceled."

There is a place for straightforward rules; sometimes we need them to hold us in check until we grasp the larger principles. We hope that as time goes on we will assimilate the principles and move on from the rules. When it comes to handling wealth in a God-honoring way, some have grasped and applied the principles, while others haven't learned the rules. Call them rules or principles—whichever suits you best.

DON'T #1: DON'T BUY WHAT YOU CAN'T AFFORD.
This can be tough. Advertisers have become so proficient at identifying our insecurities and playing to them that they can scratch us where we don't even know we itch, persuading us that we owe it to ourselves to purchase what we didn't know we needed. They know we want to be seen as attractive, to sleep like babies, to live like kings, and to vacation like movie stars. They tell us that the right clothes, the ideal car, the correct address, and the appropriate deodorant will do the trick. Before we know it we're up to our eyeballs in debt, and the advertisers and retailers are laughing their merry way to the bank with money we didn't have. A word from ancient wisdom will help:

Of what use is money in the hand of a fool,
since he has no desire to get wisdom?
PROVERBS 17:16

An old friend came to visit Jill and me in our home in England. He was a Cambridge graduate, an accomplished athlete, and a potential missionary. But he was strapped for money. He believed the Lord was calling him to Borneo, but he had no way of raising the necessary finances. My wife was consoling him shortly before he was due to leave. As he talked earnestly about his financial problems, Jill introduced a little spirituality into the conversation and assured him that if the Lord wanted him on the mission field, she had no doubt he would provide. Our friend looked out of our kitchen window at his shiny red sports car and said morosely, "I think he did—and look what I did with it!" A few minutes later he left our home with a great roar of engine, spinning wheels, and a cloud of dust. Not ten minutes elapsed before he returned, on foot, and sheepishly informed us that he had misjudged the sharp turn over the ancient bridge near our home; one side of the bridge and both sides of his car were no more! There had been some foolish expenditures in his past, but he accumulated a little wisdom en route to the bridge and eventually arrived in Borneo.

DON'T #2: DON'T BORROW WHAT YOU CAN'T REPAY.

When I first started to earn my living, I was a banker. In that noble profession I learned some good rules from the banker's point of view. I learned not to lend to people who had inadequate means of repayment. I learned not to lend to people who were incapable of posting collateral. I learned not to lend to people whose character had cracks in it—such as unreliability, untruthfulness, lack of commitment, and laziness—to mention a few. The result was that we had very few bad loans. Business flourished, and everybody agreed that we had a win/win situation.

Somewhere along the line, after I departed the profession, banking took a turn for the worse. (Not that there is any connection between my departure and the profession's problems!) Bad debts accumulated, bad loans proliferated, and bad bankers were incarcerated. The banking profession seemed to have abandoned sound principles of lending and borrowing. The results were chaos and ruin, from the international banks that folded to people who went bankrupt.

I do not subscribe to the belief that all borrowing is prohibited in Scripture. I know that Proverbs reminds us that:

The rich rule over the poor,
and the borrower is servant to the lender.
PROVERBS 22:7

But that does not put a taboo on borrowing. Scripture does, in fact, endorse borrowing and lending in some instances but warns against usury and the abuse of the needy.

A little history is in order on this point. While the nations surrounding Israel were known to charge interest at rates varying from 20–50 percent, Israelites were forbidden to charge interest on their loans to fellow Israelites. They were allowed to charge reasonable interest to non-Israelites and were encouraged to lend to the needy. We must also remember that Israel had not developed a banking system—that came much later from the merchants of Lombard, Italy.

As for application, one foolproof way of getting debt under control is to get rid of as many credit cards as possible. Have plastic surgery—get your credit cards cut off!

DON'T #3: DON'T GUARANTEE WHAT YOU ARE NOT PREPARED TO PAY.
A friend in great financial straits asks you to guarantee a loan, helping him out of a financial hole. The friend assures you that you only have to sign a note and that will be the end of it. So in good faith you sign on the dotted line. But that is not the end of it; the lender calls upon you to pay what was promised when your friend fails to do so.

Lots of people have been in this embarrassing situation. If you are not willing to say good-bye to some of your hard-earned pennies, then heed the word of the Lord:

> *My son, if you have put up security for your neighbor,*
> *if you have struck hands in pledge for another,*
> *if you have been trapped by what you said,*
> *ensnared by the words of your mouth,*
> *then do this, my son, to free yourself,*
> *since you have fallen into your neighbor's hands:*
> *Go and humble yourself;*
> *press your plea with your neighbor!*
> *Allow no sleep to your eyes,*
> *no slumber to your eyelids.*
> *Free yourself, like a gazelle from the hand of the hunter,*
> *like a bird from the snare of the fowler.*
> PROVERBS 6:1-5

There is nothing God-honoring about silly buying, stupid borrowing, or second-guess guaranteeing. It is more honorable to establish and live by sound principles, even if it means saying "no" to a "friend."

2. Maintaining healthy perspectives.

Bold type grabs our attention, while small print strains the eyes. Never is this more true than in the offers of instant riches that find their way into our homes. The dazzling possibilities of living in the lap of luxury, of opportunities that boggle the mind and stretch our horizons, have been known to hypnotize even the most levelheaded person, so much so that they never read the small print. So let's read the small print; let's make sure we keep a healthy perspective on money. Remember three things:

- Money brings its own problems;
- Money has built-in limitations; and
- Money can't purchase the main things.

PERSPECTIVE #1: MONEY BRINGS ITS OWN PROBLEMS.

A lot of people believe that a little more money will solve their problems. This may be true, but more money will also introduce new problems. Getting rid of the old problems may be a relief, but the new problems may be worse.

> *A man's riches may ransom his life,*
> *but a poor man hears no threat.*
>
> PROVERBS 13:8

I love that one! It's a bad news/good news proverb. First the bad news: "A man's riches may ransom his life." This means that if you're a rich man, somebody may kidnap you. That's the bad news! Now the good news: If you're rich you may be able to pay the ransom. The bad news for the poor man is—he's broke. The good news is that he's so broke, nobody is going to kidnap him! So what's better? To be rich enough to pay off your kidnapper or to be so poor that no self-respecting kidnapper would give you a second look?

Maybe we shouldn't automatically assume that rich is always better. I once saw an embroidered cushion in the home of friends that said, "I've been poor, and I've been rich. Rich is better." Maybe so, but it would not be wise to assume that money solves all problems. It doesn't, because it has problems of its own.

PERSPECTIVE #2: MONEY HAS BUILT-IN LIMITATIONS.

Wealth is worthless in the day of wrath.
PROVERBS 11:4

This is one of the most chilling, realistic statements on money you'll read anywhere. It is possible that the day of wrath referred to here is the day of your neighbor's anger. If your neighbor is really mad, your money won't calm him down. In fact, given the love affair with litigation in our culture, it could be that money is not only incapable of assuaging someone's anger, but it also may incite them to sue you.

More likely, however, the day of wrath is the Day of Judgment, when the dead, small and great, will stand before God and give an account of their lives. On that great and solemn day, money won't help a bit. The currency of this world is not legal tender in eternity. While financial assets can get you the best attorney that money can buy and the best deal the law allows, when your day in eternal court comes, money won't help.

PERSPECTIVE #3: MONEY CAN'T PURCHASE THE MAIN THINGS.

*Better a little with the fear of the LORD
than great wealth with turmoil.*
PROVERBS 15:16

As we have seen, "the fear of the Lord is the beginning of wisdom." This rule is foundational to an eternally worthwhile life. It is more valuable than anything else in the world. Better to be at peace with the Lord, to have a sense of pleasing and honoring him, and be lacking in financial resources, than to be loaded with assets and bowed down with a crushing load of inner turmoil.

A good name is more desirable than great riches;
to be esteemed is better than silver or gold.

PROVERBS 22:1

The people of Israel had the double responsibility to love the Lord and to love their neighbors. Life was to be lived on both vertical and horizontal planes. Fearing the Lord was, therefore, quite naturally paired with having a good name.

Today, being respected and being seen as people of integrity are still significant. Many people do not believe this until it is too late. They are so enamored with wealth and the power and privilege that come with it that they forget about the image they are projecting. Not a few celebrities have found that while their investments were paying great dividends, their stock was taking a beating. There has been a sad procession of the rich and famous who have finished up with resources intact but reputations in tatters.

3. Developing appropriate procedures.

Once we have seen that "all that glitters is not gold," we are in a position to handle our resources with common sense, even to the point of establishing procedures that will carry out in practice what we believe in principle. The book of Proverbs is not at all reticent to come up with straightforward instructions.

PROCEDURE #1: USE WEALTH IN WORSHIP.

Honor the LORD with your wealth,
with the firstfruits of all your crops.

PROVERBS 3:9

Those for whom these Proverbs were originally written presented their offerings to the Lord in the course of their normal worship experience. They lived in an agrarian culture; their income was tied to flocks and crops. So as soon as they reaped their harvest, they took the first sheaf to the temple, and there they offered it before the Lord. They took the firstborn of all their flocks to the priests, and they actually committed the firstborn of their children to the service of the Lord.

These were *firstfruits*. As God stipulated to the people of Israel, that offering was not to be whatever was left over after they had pleased themselves. In fact, they worshiped God right off the top—with *firstfruits*.

As a small boy I remember watching my father, who owned a grocery store, counting his earnings at the end of the day. I noticed that he put most of the money in one cash box and a smaller amount in another box. When I asked him why he did that he explained, "Stuart, everything we have belongs to the Lord and he asks us to show that we understand that by giving back a portion to him and his work. If we don't do that it means we are keeping for ourselves that which really belongs to God. That's called stealing. So to make sure that does not happen, each day at the end of the day we put the Lord's portion in this box. It is his—not ours!"

The right way to give to the Lord is to present *first*fruits—off the top—rather than leftovers—off the bottom. If you establish a budget—a very good idea—you can ensure that giving has its rightful place by making the top item on your lists of expenses "Giving." That was basically what my Dad was doing, except he used a tin box. Today he would probably use a computer program, with the same priorities firmly established.

PROCEDURE #2: USE WEALTH FOR YOUR FAMILY.

In the house of the wise are stores of choice food and oil,
but a foolish man devours all he has.
PROVERBS 21:20

Giving to the Lord must not be at the expense of family. There is nothing God-honoring about a family that is neglected in the name

of serving the Lord. He is served in the family as surely as he is worshiped in the sanctuary. Properly administered resources will lead to
adequately cared-for families. Families are cared for when there is
concern for their future as well as their present.

This was particularly important for the people of Israel because
their continued presence in the Land of Promise was part of God's
covenant with them. At any given moment their hold on the territory
was tenuous because of the presence of their enemies. So prudent
families looked to the future and found ways to make it secure. The
modern practice of mortgaging the future is far from biblical and has
little to commend it from a practical point of view.

A good man leaves an inheritance for his children's children.

PROVERBS 13:22

PROCEDURE #3: USE WEALTH FOR THOSE WHO ARE IN NEED.

The righteous give without sparing.

PROVERBS 21:26

A generous man will prosper;
he who refreshes others will himself be refreshed.

PROVERBS 11:25

John Wesley wrote, "Make as much as you can; save as much as you
can; give as much as you can." That is about as balanced a view of
money as I've seen. It reflects a proper attitude toward productivity,
toward prudence, and toward philanthropy. And when those three
are in balance, it is evidence of a balanced life. A person's biography is
often written in large letters in his bank statement and engraved on
his credit cards.

THE SLIP-SLIDING SOCIETY

We seem to be hovering on the very brink of disaster,
not only from international conflict but from the internal incoherence
of our own society. What has gone wrong? How can we reverse
the slide toward the abyss?

ROBERT BELLAH

s I write, two epochal events in American history are being commemorated. The sixtieth anniversary of Japan's infamous attack on Pearl Harbor on December 7, 1941 and the three month "anniversary" of the wicked attacks on the World Trade Center and the Pentagon in Washington, D.C., on September 11, 2001. The former thrust America into the Second World War with results that changed the face of Europe; the latter precipitated the United States' entry into the War on Terrorism, the results of which are yet to be spelled out in the years to come.

The immediate response to the events of 9/11 included a surge in church attendance and in Bible sales. People turned to prayer in great numbers. American flags appeared on boulevards, porches, and lapels. Firefighters and policemen turned into overnight heroes. Politicians declared a kind of truce as they stood shoulder to shoulder with the president, who himself rode a new surge in unprecedented popularity after a shaky start to his presidency. Men remembered to kiss their wives goodbye before leaving for work, and many found time to

run their kids to school. A spirit of goodwill which we normally experience briefly over the Christmas period became apparent. People expressed solidarity with the victims of the attacks with huge donations
of blood and money. Even children donated millions of dollars to the
needy children of Afghanistan.

I said "the immediate response" for a very good reason. While reactions to the traumatic events were real and striking, many of them
were apparently shallow and superficial, because just three months after the events, people were returning to "normal." This is certainly
true of church attendance in general, which has returned to similar
percentages to the previous December, and of prayer meetings in particular, where mostly it is the faithful few who show up to pray. The
Barna Research Group reported that there was no discernible change
in people's religious beliefs and behaviors with the startling exceptions that fewer people believed in moral absolutes or the existence of
Satan after the attacks than before! Politicians got back to quibbling
about the things they usually quibble about; arguments have erupted
about the way the charitable donations are being administered. It
now appears that most of the donated blood was not needed, and the
spirit of goodwill and community is showing signs of wear and tear.

Under stress human beings betray a spiritual instinct. In the same
way that there are reputedly no atheists in foxholes, so during times of
traumatic upheaval people, in their insecurity, look instinctively for
help and support from a "higher power." Do you remember the man
who prayed, "God, get me out of this and I'll never bother you again"?
God did his part and the man was as good as his word! When under attack people look for heroes and symbols of strength, and they herd together for hope and help. We saw all these things, and it is encouraging
to see this side of human nature. Spiritual instincts, community spirit,
neighborliness, the recognition and affirmation of values like courage
and faithfulness, perseverance and self-sacrifice, patriotism and service,
and kindness and generosity were all there in abundance.

But all these began to disappear in an alarmingly short space of time. In the aftermath of 9/11, Hollywood showed considerable concern by debating whether the type of films they had been making were suitable any more. But they quickly regained their normal posture! Robert Redford told us that the American people needed to understand the inner workings of the CIA at this time when they were in action in Afghanistan, and therefore, he believed that his movie, *Spy Game*, should be shown. Shown it was, and what it showed was "nothing has changed." For Redford plays the part of a retiring CIA agent who, on his last day at work, is faced with a predicament that he solves by all manner of slick, sly, wicked-grin-on-the-face means. In no uncertain terms he shows that "the brass" that insists on doing things by the book are stupid and inept, and people like him, who cut the corners, are the ones who make things happen. Good-bye heroes and welcome back antiheroes! The movie that Redford had portrayed as significant, helpful, and needful was in actuality a sham. It portrayed a cynical disregard for true values and a smooth misrepresentation of a national institution. What a turnaround in less than three months!

Deep down in the human soul, there are longings and aspirations that are gracious and noble and good and right. But instincts that are divisive, disruptive, destructive, and devilish combat and contradict the good. And our culture is showing the strain.

Jimmy Carter talked about a "national malaise" and was roundly ridiculed for it. But Dr. Robert Bellah and his colleagues, respected California sociologists, after making a scholarly study of American social mores, said similar things and people listened. They wrote in *Habits of the Heart*:

> For over a hundred years, a large part of the American people, the middle class, has imagined that the virtual meaning of life lies in the acquisition of ever increasing status, income and authority, from which genuine

freedom is supposed to come. Our achievements have been enormous. They permit us the aspiration to become a genuinely humane society in a genuinely decent world and provide many of the means to attain that aspiration. Yet we seem to be hovering on the very brink of disaster, not only from international conflict but from the internal incoherence of our own society. What has gone wrong? How can we reverse the slide toward the abyss?[41]

Fundamentalist preachers talk quite often about halting a slide toward an abyss—or words to that effect—but rarely southern California sociologists. Dr. Bellah and his team were very straightforward in their statements. They go on:

> Our society has been deeply influenced by the tradition of modern individualism. We have taken the position that our most important task today is the recovery of the insights of the older biblical . . . traditions.[42]

When I hear that sort of thing, I get excited. But let me back up a little bit.

THE MAKINGS OF A NATION

In the beginning of American society, there were three central cultural strands, like a rope of three strands. *Habits of the Heart* called them biblical, republican, and individualistic.

Biblical Beginnings

The biblical strand refers to the profound influence of such early Americans as the Pilgrim Fathers. They believed fervently in a sovereign God, and they left Europe and came to America believing that they had the opportunity to establish a new society based on biblical principles. One of their leaders, John Winthrop, the first governor of Massachusetts, said, "We must delight in each other, make others' conditions our own, rejoice together, mourn together, labor and suffer together, always having before our eyes . . . our community as members of the same body."[43]

These noble sentiments sprang from the Bible, which they loved to read and sought to obey. They were convinced that it gave them the Lord's instruction as to how to run their lives and their state.

Republican Rationales

This is not Republican as opposed to Democrat, but rather republican as opposed to monarchist. One of the reasons the colonists left England and came to the New World was that they didn't like living under a monarchy. They were less than enthusiastic about being told what to do by someone whose only authority appeared to be derived from the accident of his birth as the firstborn of privileged parents—who had become sovereigns for similar or even less compelling reasons. Republicans believed that they should be involved in the choice of their leaders.

One of the people who advocated this approach was Thomas Jefferson. He insisted that all people are created equal and that all these people had the right, privilege, and responsibility to be involved in the affairs of the state. He even went so far as to say, "Love your neighbor as yourself and your country more than yourself"—a good example of his disconcerting habit of rewriting, amplifying, or editing Scripture to suit his own purposes!

Individualistic Inclinations

Benjamin Franklin was a great example of the much-admired American self-made man—the rugged individual, the one who, born in the land of the free and the home of the brave, had been free enough and brave enough to make something out of his life because he was born in the land of opportunity and made the most of it. Franklin was the quintessential poor boy who made good. Born the son of a soap and candle maker, he showed great aptitude in his youth. He was apprenticed to a printer and eventually started his own printing business. By the time he was in his early forties, he had made his fortune and was able to retire and devote his attention to publishing, to writing *Poor Richard's Almanac,* and to scientific experimentation—not to mention, of course, politics and intrigue. This was a man who had taken the initiative and made something of himself, an individualist.

Even a cursory glance at contemporary society will show that the biblical and the republican strands have become severely frayed. We have moved farther from the individual committed to working for the good of society and toward the individual committed to the good of the self. The abyss of which the sociologists were speaking is the possibility that our culture may become less and less viable as we lose our biblical moorings, disregard our sense of communal responsibility, and move farther away from a desire to develop God-given abilities, preferring to squander our lives on self-gratification.

BIBLICAL VALUES TO STAND ON

Let love and faithfulness never leave you;
bind them around your neck,
write them on the tablet of your heart.
Then you will win favor and a good name
in the sight of God and man.

PROVERBS 3:3-4

He who pursues righteousness and love
finds life, prosperity, and honor.

PROVERBS 21:21

Anything that produces a lifestyle that both God and man esteem highly is not only unusual but also desirable and commendable. And here we see that love and faithfulness result in this kind of approval. Love, faithfulness, and righteousness show up consistently throughout Scripture as God reveals his own character to us. These then, are three biblical values that should be foundational to our personal and community value systems.

Love

The Hebrew word for "love" used throughout the Old Testament is *hesed*. It has various connotations. It means, first of all, a steadfast commitment. Modern thinking tends to emphasize love's emotional dimension, but the biblical understanding of love concentrates more on commitment. The *hesed* of God puts more emphasis on decision than emotion, although, of course it contains an emotional aspect. The best demonstration of this is in God's decision to make a covenant with the people of Israel. He freely chose to do this, and he was at great pains to remind the covenant people that it was not because of who they were that he had been attracted to them and had chosen to love them. He told them quite bluntly that they were not a particularly winsome or promising group at all. His *hesed* was a matter of what he chose to do and not a matter of what they deserved to receive.

The second characteristic of love, as seen in the character of God, is a moral obligation to another's well-being. Over and over again the prophets reminded the people of Israel that God was totally committed and morally obligated to work for their well-being. Micah the prophet understood this and expressed it beautifully:

> *Who is a God like you,*
> *who pardons sin and forgives the transgression*
> *of the remnant of his inheritance?*
> *You do not stay angry forever*
> *but delight to show mercy [hesed].*
> *You will again have compassion on us;*
> *you will tread our sins underfoot*

and hurl our iniquities into the depths of the sea.
You will be true to Jacob,
and show mercy [hesed] to Abraham,
as you pledged on oath to our fathers in days long ago.

MICAH 7:18-20

How could God, who had "pledged on oath" based on love, ever renege on his commitment? It was unthinkable. Micah knew that a loving God could be counted on to be "true to Jacob." His love was a moral obligation to follow through on what he had promised.

The third characteristic of God's love is a strong initiative of kindness, tenderness, and compassion. You may remember that when Moses asked God for a revelation of himself, the Lord said, "The LORD, the LORD, the compassionate and gracious God, slow to anger, abounding in love and faithfulness, maintaining love to thousands, and forgiving wickedness, rebellion and sin" (Exod. 34:6-7). Love is mentioned there twice in conjunction with such wonderful words as *compassionate, gracious, patience* (or "slow to anger"), *faithful,* and *forgiving.* When you put all those words together, you get a picture of the love of God.

We are to pursue this kind of love! We are not to derive our idea of love from ourselves, nor are we to understand it as portrayed in our society. Love, God's style, has the ability to build up our society rather than tear it down. This kind of love is a steadfast commitment that springs from moral obligation and is demonstrated by strong initiatives of kindness, tenderness, and compassion.

Think of the difference these values would make in today's distressed world. Think of the frayed strands of our cultural rope and of what could happen if we recovered this old biblical tradition.

Faithfulness

Faithfulness, also, is rooted in the character of God. Faithfulness is defined as "a determined loyalty to a covenant." Once again we must refer to the covenant God made with Israel. He did not make a contract. A contract says, "I will do this, and you are required to do that." A covenant says, "I commit myself to doing this. I assume and I trust and I hope and I long for a valid response from you, but my covenant is a commitment, and I will be determinedly loyal to that commitment."

In the book of Lamentations there's a famous phrase, "Great is thy faithfulness," that has been made into a hymn, which we sing with great gusto. Have you ever read that statement in its context? The author of Lamentations—traditionally Jeremiah—was deploring the devastation of Jerusalem and the decimation of God's people. But in the midst of his anguish he says:

> *Because of the LORD's great love we are not consumed,*
> *for his compassions never fail.*
> *They are new every morning;*
> *great is your faithfulness.*

LAMENTATIONS 3:22-23

Jeremiah was able to see that even in the midst of unmitigated disaster, Israel could count on the unchanging loyalty of God toward his commitment. This is the essence of faithfulness.

How many truly faithful people have you known? What kind of difference would it make if you were known to be completely faithful, a person who always followed through on commitments, someone who would rather take a loss or be inconvenienced than go back on his or her word?

We live in a society that is shot through with mistrust and fear. We are actually surprised when people do what they say they will do, when they say they will do it. If we talk on the phone to a business, we have learned to get the name of the contact person, because we know that when we call again (when what we hoped would have been taken care of hasn't been taken care of), another person will answer, and no one will know what we are talking about. No one is accountable. People are hesitant to take responsibility; they refer us elsewhere or patch us through to the voice mail of someone at another level of the process. And we haven't even touched the area of faithfulness in friendship and in marriage. How refreshing it would be if faithfulness, that old-fashioned biblical value, became valuable to a majority of the people with whom we work and live.

Righteousness

Righteousness in the Old Testament, strictly speaking, means "the fulfillment of the expectations of a relationship." God's righteousness is demonstrated in his always being and doing what he has promised to be and do in any relationship that he initiates. So when Moses was getting the people ready to enter the Land of Promise, he reminisced in a song about all the ways that God had dealt with his people in bringing them out of Egypt and leading them through the wilderness. He wrote:

> *I will proclaim the name of the LORD.*
> *Oh, praise the greatness of our God!*
> *He is the Rock, his works are perfect,*
> *and all his ways are just.*
> *A faithful God who does no wrong,*
> *upright and just is he.*
> DEUTERONOMY 32:3-4

Moses emphasizes that God has been faithful, upright, and just in all his dealings with the people of Israel. In his turbulent relationship with his truculent people, God had always acted rightly!

PUTTING VALUES INTO PRACTICE
Acting Lovingly

> *Many a man claims to have unfailing love [hesed],*
> *but a faithful man who can find?*
> PROVERBS 20:6

Now that is downright discouraging, but it is also very realistic. It is relatively easy for us to proclaim unfailing love—we do it in every wedding ceremony—but it's an entirely different matter for us to produce it. In fact, if the truth were known, we have an inherent inability to produce that kind of love and faithfulness. There is something unloving, unfaithful, and unrighteous about us as human beings. Nevertheless, there is something in the human heart that longs for love—the kind that is reliable and faithful. Proverbs says as much:

What a man desires is unfailing love [hesed].
PROVERBS 19:22

The Revised Standard Version translates the verse, "What is desired in a man is loyalty." People want us not only to be loving toward them, but also to be loyal. But I find a tension within me. I recognize my inherent inability to love that way, but I have a desire to do it, and people desire this kind of love from me. What can I do?

The answer is that we need to recognize our own deficiencies in love and faithfulness, face up to our failings—our "falling short" of God's standards (Rom. 3:23)—and seek God to have our sins forgiven and our lives changed.

He who conceals his sins does not prosper,
but whoever confesses and renounces them finds mercy.
PROVERBS 28:13

Through love and faithfulness sin is atoned for;
through the fear of the LORD a man avoids evil.
PROVERBS 16:6

When we operate on divine principles, we will avoid evil. If and when we lapse into unloving, unfaithful, unrighteous actions, we come before the Lord in repentance and seek his forgiveness, and he works a change in our lives. And because of his love and faithfulness, we then have the power to express love and faithfulness.

Those who plan what is good find [or "show"]
love and faithfulness.

PROVERBS 14:22

When confronted with our failure, it is very easy for us to simply shrug our shoulders and say, "I'm only human. Everybody else is doing it, and my problem with being loving and faithful are rooted in my childhood, and there's no way I can expect to change at this late stage." But no! Those who do what is right according to God's standards and avail themselves of the spiritual resources he provides for them will find and demonstrate love and faithfulness.

The papers are full of sickening stories of ten- and eleven-year-old boys murdering old ladies, of children bearing babies, and children who blow other children away. One wonders at a society that has sunk so low that children lack moral sensitivity, qualifying for life in prison before they have graduated from junior high school; a society where home and family have deteriorated to such an extent that children grow up influenced by all that is evil and corrupt around them rather than by that which is wholesome and healthy; a society where the downward drag of sin has no counteracting dynamic to lift young people to higher planes; a culture where leaders bemoan the state of home and family, of inner city and outlying suburb, but appear impotent to bring about change. What's wrong?

That's the question Robert Bellah and his colleagues asked as they looked at the "abyss." They knew that a return to the old biblical values was urgently and desperately called for—a reintroduction of God's kind of love. And that doesn't start with a nationwide government- sponsored program; it begins with a revolution of love in my heart and yours.

Acting Faithfully

In our litigious culture, where a woman who spills her coffee over herself not only has the audacity to sue McDonald's but actually wins and walks away a millionaire, we don't think much of covenants.

We prefer contracts, those that are negotiable if the time comes that we think the contract we freely agreed to is no longer to our advantage. So it is normal for a highly paid athlete to negotiate a contract, find out someone else is earning more, refuse to honor the agreement, and refuse to play until his contract is renegotiated. I am waiting for the day when an athlete negotiates a contract, has a bad year the following season, and returns his bloated earnings with a note to the effect that he doesn't deserve that kind of money, he hasn't earned it, and it should be given to someone who has produced! And he would like his contract renegotiated to reflect his lack of production. I'm not holding my breath!

We have all heard of or attended incredibly sentimental, romantic weddings where great promises of fidelity were made only to be broken almost before the ink was dry on the wedding certificate. Some people, wise to that possibility, have shown their uneasiness about the character of the person they are marrying by insisting on a prenuptial agreement that, in effect, invalidates the essence of the vows they are about to take.

Let's take a look at how things could and should be:

> *Like the coolness of snow at harvest time*
> *is a trustworthy messenger to those who send him;*
> *he refreshes the spirit of his masters.*
> PROVERBS 25:13

Here the word *trustworthy* is related to faithfulness. There is something refreshing about somebody who promises and follows through. It ought to be so commonplace that it is not so noteworthy, but in a culture where people expect, for very good reasons, to be ripped off, a person who acts upon principles of reliability, trustworthiness, and honesty is unusual.

When Robertson McQuilkin resigned as president of Columbia Bible College and Seminary after his wife, Muriel, was diagnosed as having Alzheimer's disease, he explained that she had cared for him as she had promised; now it was his turn to care for her as he had promised. So extraordinary did his action appear, even though it was not at all unusual, given the marital vows they had made to each other long years before, that he was deluged by surprised responses. From Christians! Even the church got a shock when a man did what was right rather than what was easy—for no other reason than that he had said he would.

There is an obvious connection between truth and trust and between trustworthiness and truthfulness. Faithfulness is behind all of them. The faithful don't betray trust, and they do project truth. But breaking contracts has become normal; telling lies has reached epidemic proportions.

> *The LORD detests lying lips,*
> *but he delights in men who are truthful.*
>
> PROVERBS 12:22

Faithful people will be committed to truthfulness, they will say exactly what they mean, they will mean what they say, and they will stick with it. The Lord delights in this kind of person—he himself is faithful and truthful. And it is no surprise that he detests lying lips.

Lying has almost become a normative way of doing business. For many people lying is part of the way they relate to each other. Some lie to save another person's feelings. "I just love your dress," they say, when they're thinking, *Why in the world would she wear that?* More serious is the habit of lying to save your own skin. We learn to do this early on when we tell the teacher, "The dog ate my homework." The practice goes on into high school and college, into job training and business, and into management. Then there's the lie that is told in order to gain the upper hand—the intention is to deceive or to cheat in order to gain something that you do not deserve and would in no other circumstances ever gain.

The place of lying in our culture was highlighted when *Time* magazine devoted a cover article to the subject. The article concluded, "Lies flourish in social uncertainty when people no longer understand, or agree on, the rules governing their behavior toward one another. During such periods skepticism also increases; there will be the perception that more people are lying, whether or not they actually are."[44]

The December 17, 2001, issue of the *Chicago Tribune* ran an article by their "cultural critic" with the headline: "George O'Leary, fired as Notre Dame's football coach, lied about his academic and athletic background." The headline was followed in even larger letters with the question, "Should that matter?" One professor of philosophy found it "fascinating" that we found his lying "so upsetting." Numerous voices were raised, according to the article, protesting, "Cut the guy some slack. It's a tough and competitive world out there and everybody lies a little. Right?" One writer said that he could not understand what a "20-year-old cushion on a resumé has to do with being the head football coach of Notre Dame." Fortunately a prominent ethicist helped him understand by explaining, "Once you get on the road to trying to get something by cheating, you are in effect giving up whatever claim you have to integrity. Its only a matter of time before you lose credibility." What is surprising is not that he lied—resumés frequently depart from the truth—or that he was fired by Notre Dame—that is one institution that still has ethical standards. What is surprising is that the question "Should that matter?" was asked. It is an example of how lying has come to be regarded as normal—"no big deal"—because "everybody does it."

Acting Rightly

Righteousness is fulfilling the expectations of a relationship. But by whose expectations do we evaluate our fulfillment? As most of us have found out from bitter experience, you may be able to please some people some of the time, but it is impossible to please all people all of the time.

Here again, our only source must be the sovereign Lord and not our own opinion or a poll of society. We may be able to convince ourselves that our actions are right because "everybody else is doing it," because it feels good, or because it achieves the desired objective. But these criteria are not adequate if we have a relationship with God. It is his expectations that really matter.

> *Righteousness and justice are the foundation of your throne;*
> *love and faithfulness go before you.*
>
> PSALM 89:14

Once our righteousness has been established before God by his grace, we embark on a lifestyle of fulfilling his expectations—not only in our relationship with him, but in all our relationships. He created us to have relationships in the first place, and he also designed right ways of relating. Scripture is full of information that helps us with our relationships. Marriage and family are two areas in which he has invested particular care and attention.

In counseling young couples I have found that many of their marital problems stem from unmet expectations. Sometimes the expectations have not been articulated; at other times they are totally unrealistic. Expectations can be a minefield because we may not know they are there until we step on them and they blow up in our face! If marriage partners and family members can agree that God's standards and expectations are the right ones, they will establish common ground and will have a much better chance of arriving at common goals.

I know a young couple whose marriage was in deep trouble. There had been serious failure by both partners. Tempers were frayed, recriminations were flying around, and the possibility of salvaging anything from the disastrous situation was remote. But there was one saving grace: Both parties knew what was right. Some people were encouraging them to do what they wanted; others told them to look out for number one; still others advised them to take each other to the cleaners. But they both knew what was right. In the end, in spite of everything, they made a hard-nosed decision to do what was right. Many of the people who had been involved in the situation were amazed when the couple made a commitment to do what they really didn't want to do, going against the advice of almost everybody. They decided to recommit to each other, to forgive each other, and to do it for no other reason than that it was the right thing to do according to their understanding of God's ways. It was not easy, and everything was not perfect, but they battled through and not only had the deep-rooted joy of knowing they had done the right thing, but they also discovered reserves of strength they did not know they possessed and depths of love they had never imagined.

Former president Jimmy Carter made a genuine attempt to do the right thing as president—and he paid a high price for trying. On one occasion during his presidency, a vote at the United Nations was cast wrongly. The world was startled, but it was obviously a mistake. When the president was informed, he instructed that the mistake should be admitted and the vote recast. His advisers pointed out, however, that the president was being widely criticized at that time for being indecisive—for flip-flopping—and that to change the vote would be political suicide. Better, in their opinion, to leave the vote alone, even though it was wrong, and ride out the storm. President Carter, however, to his credit—and to his political deficit—insisted that the vote be changed for no other reason than it was wrong. He was committed to doing what was right, not what was expedient. That kind of attitude may have cost him the presidency, but I doubt it ever cost him a night's sleep.

There is something refreshing about honesty in an age of shady deals. It's always uplifting to hear truth spoken in an environment of lies and half-truths. When people do what is right rather than settling for what is comfortable, profitable, or popular, there is hope. It's that kind of righteousness that exalts a nation.

> *When the righteous thrive, the people rejoice;*
> *when the wicked rule, the people groan.*
> PROVERBS 29:2

Acting Justly
Standing for what is right at times will mean taking a stand for justice or taking the side of the underprivileged. We need only turn to Proverbs or the book of Amos.

> *The righteous care about justice for the poor,*
> *but the wicked have no such concern.*
> PROVERBS 29:7
> *You oppress the righteous and take bribes*
> *and you deprive the poor of justice in the courts.*
> *But let justice roll on like a river,*
> *righteousness like a never-failing stream!*
> AMOS 5:12, 24

What this means for the individual who takes the principle seriously will vary from one situation to another. For some it meant being active in the civil rights movement. For others it means taking action on behalf of the unborn. Still others throw themselves into relief work for Third World nations facing starvation.

NECKTIES AND NECKLACES
The more I think about the values of love, faithfulness, righteousness, and justice, the more I am forced to reevaluate my own lifestyle, the more discouraged I become about the contemporary scene, and the

more excited I am about the opportunities for radical change if only we dare to follow the old biblical values.

How can we do that? A key proverb tells us what to do.

Let love and faithfulness never leave you;
bind them about your neck,
write them on the tablet of your heart.

PROVERBS 3:3

Usually the things we tie around our necks are there either to make a statement or to add ornamentation—or both. So, for instance, in contemporary church services the minister dispenses with a tie and wears a polo shirt and thereby shows that he is in touch with the modern world. On the other hand the traditional minister will don a Roman collar or a jacket and tie and thus demonstrate to the faithful that he stands for the grand historic traditions of the church. The same is true in the business world. In Silicon Valley the young computer geniuses eschew ties and wear blue jeans and T-shirts with fashionably unlaced Nikes, while on Wall Street "power" ties and three-piece suits flourish. Whether it is the power tie, the regimental tie, the club tie, the "fish" tie, or the psychedelic tie, it makes a statement about the wearer's personality. The same can be said of necklaces. Whether the fashionable string of pearls worn with a classic black dress, or the artsy creations that originated in an obscure tribe, both are statements about the wearer.

How about this for a statement? How about getting up in the morning, going to your spiritual closet, and carefully choosing how best to "tie on" love and faithfulness before stepping out into the world? How about intentionally moving around on earth "wearing" a striking commitment to love and faithfulness? That would get noticed in the boardroom and at the cocktail hour, in the sports club and at the family table.

Writing these values on the tablet of the heart means that the words of Scripture are not to be regarded as nice sentiments but rather that they should be taken to heart. Paul used a similar idea when he said that the Corinthians were "a letter from Christ . . . written not with ink but with the Spirit of the living God, not on tablets of stone but on tablets of human hearts" (2 Cor. 3:3). In the same way that God's commandments given to Moses were put in writing on stone, so also the gospel of grace is to be written on people's hearts. This requires them to make a decision and a commitment to "love and faithfulness."

As a preacher and pastor I have often been surprised at the ease with which people can turn at the end of a service of worship to talk about trivial matters. It sometimes seems that the congregation greets the end of the service with a sense of relief and quickly adjusts to "normal life." Perhaps a more appropriate response would be to go away quietly and think of ways to apply and write on one's heart the things that have been taught. We are to bind God's principles around our necks and write them on our hearts.

> *He who pursues righteousness and love*
> *finds life, prosperity, and honor.*
> PROVERBS 21:21

Pursuit is a picture of the single-mindedness that is needed if we are to live in today's culture committed to such values as love, righteousness, and faithfulness.

Something is sadly wrong with the way our society operates. We can blame institutions and look for governmental solutions, and we may have a point. But our response to great disasters shows a desire for righteousness, love, and faithfulness—things that we manage without most of the time. Many of us were not pursuing these things on September 10, but quickly embraced them on September 11, then slipped back to old patterns with alarming alacrity. We know better, and we desire more, but we don't follow through. As a result we are diminished, relationships are damaged, and our society is in danger.

It does not have to be this way; God calls us to something grander and nobler. Through the empowering of his Spirit he makes available to us all that it takes to be all that he desires (2 Pet. 1:3). So let's avail ourselves of his gracious provision, take seriously his powerful admonitions, and see our own lives enriched and the lives of those who live within our sphere of influence immeasurably changed—for good!

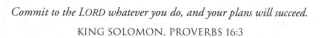

PERSONAL AMBITION

Commit to the LORD whatever you do, and your plans will succeed.

KING SOLOMON, PROVERBS 16:3

I have friends who live in Siberia. They are Christians who believe they should serve the people of that needy part of the world's largest nation. One of them told me that many of the shutters of the Siberian buildings had been painted blue and green, but all of them were in a sad state of disrepair. All the paint was peeling. He spoke to a Siberian friend about this and was told that, traditionally, the blue stood for "Hope" and the green for "Life," but as they had lost all hope and didn't have a life worth living, they had stopped painting the shutters. In Siberia the air of resigned hopelessness is written deeply on the expressionless faces of the people as they go listlessly about their lives without hope and with nothing to live for.

This state of affairs is not altogether unknown in the West. W. H. Auden captured it in his poem entitled, "September 1, 1939":

Faces along the bar
Cling to their average day;
The lights must never go out.

The music must always play
Lest we know where we are,
Lost in a haunted wood,
Children afraid of the dark,
Who have never been happy or good.[45]

There is no shortage of people in our towns, cities, and farms who cling to their average days and clutch a life-saving fifth, people who are devoid of purpose and robbed of ambition. When hope is lost and ambition has died, life becomes a burden to be borne with dull apathy, drowned in vodka, or denounced with bitterness.

In a nationwide survey conducted by the authors of *The Day Americans Told the Truth*, people were asked among other things, "If you could change one thing about yourself what would it be?" The top choice was, "My weight"; the second, "My body"; and the third, "My age." This question was followed by, "If you could change one thing about your life what would it be?" The runaway favorite answer was, "I would like to have more money."[46]

Do these answers suggest that the people interviewed entertained grand ambitions and noble aspirations? Weight, body, age, and money—little about those things is spiritual and eternal. But they are in the forefront of people's interest and apparently portray the depth of their ambitions.

If Edmund Burke were alive today, he would not be surprised by these answers. Mr. Burke wrote, "Well is it known that ambition can creep as well as soar."[47] Purely material ambitions tend to be creepy! Burke's contention was that Oliver Cromwell's Puritan convictions were initially at the fore, and he acted accordingly. You could say his ambitions soared! Based on what he learned from the Bible, Cromwell made decisions that were sound and healthy. But as time went on another kind of ambition—personal, material ambition that crept—took over and "suspended" his spiritual convictions. As a result Cromwell made decisions that were clearly out of line with those convictions, bringing much pain and suffering to England.

Ambition, that powerful driving force that everybody possesses in varying degrees, should have spiritual underpinnings. Sadly, some ambitions owe nothing to spiritual considerations and others, once noble and soaring, descend into lower, creeping postures as spiritual considerations are suspended in the search for personal gain, fame, vindication, or satisfaction.

We need to look for ambitions that soar. And here again the book of Proverbs comes to our aid.

> *The fear of the LORD teaches a man wisdom,*
> *and humility comes before honor.*
> *To man belong the plans of the heart,*
> *but from the LORD comes the reply of the tongue.*
> *All a man's ways seem innocent to him,*
> *but motives are weighed by the LORD.*
> *Commit to the LORD whatever you do,*
> *and your plans will succeed.*
> *The LORD works out everything for his own ends—*
> *even the wicked for a day of disaster.*
> *The LORD detests all the proud of heart.*
> *Be sure of this: They will not go unpunished.*
> *Through love and faithfulness sin is atoned for;*
> *through the fear of the LORD a man avoids evil.*
> *When a man's ways are pleasing to the LORD,*
> *he makes even his enemies live at peace with him.*
>
> PROVERBS 15:33—16:7

This striking passage begins with a reminder concerning the fear of the Lord and ends with a promise concerning pleasing the Lord. You could say that the *fear of the Lord* is the basis of our decision making, and *pleasing the Lord* is the end that we keep in mind—our overriding ambition.

AMBITION TO PLEASE THE LORD

The ultimate value for which we should aim, our noblest aspiration, is not that we should please ourselves, nor even that we should please the community of which we are a part, but that we should be pleasing to the sovereign God who made us. That should be our ambition. But how do we go about pleasing the Lord?

Embracing Divine Principles

As surely as there are physical laws in our material world, there are spiritual laws that we ignore at our own peril. There are certain prerequisites to what we like to think of as "the good life." But those prerequisites are surprisingly different from what we might expect. There are many paradoxes in God's divine system of cause and effect. If we are to enjoy the fulfillment he designed us to enjoy, we will need to understand and apply his universal principles.

PRINCIPLE #1: HUMILITY COMES BEFORE HONOR.

The ancient Greeks, who studied virtues at great length, did not include humility in their list of desirable traits. They regarded humility as demeaning, and they much preferred pride. But the ancient Hebrews *did* regard humility as a virtue.

What does humility really mean? The word humility literally means "lowliness of mind." Charles Haddon Spurgeon said that humility is the ability to make a right assessment of oneself. Paul told the people of the church in Rome, "Do not think of yourself more highly than you ought, but rather think of yourself with sober judgment, in accordance with the measure of faith God has given you" (Rom. 12:3). The operative words here appear to be "more highly," suggesting that it is possible to think highly, not highly enough, or too highly of oneself. Robert Burns, the Scottish poet, exclaimed:

Oh would some Power the gift give us
To see ourselves as others see us![48]

There's no question that the insights of other people can be a helpful addition to our own perceptions of self. However, other people have their own prejudices, preconceptions, and problems that may affect the way they see you. Other people's glasses are at best tinted, at worst warped. The thing that we really need is the ability to see ourselves as God sees us. The extent to which we can do that will determine the degree to which we can gain what Spurgeon called "a right assessment" of self.

Once we see ourselves as God sees us, we will be well on the road to humility. Why? Because we are God's creatures and he is the Creator. In realizing that we are the created, we must recognize that both our existence and survival depend on our Creator. And if we the creatures recognize that we have failed to meet our obligations to the Creator, we will experience a sense of having fallen short. If we know in our hearts that we have failed to be all that we were created to be, we will recognize the need to relate not only as creature to Creator, but also as sinner to offended deity. These insights lead us to humility.

PRINCIPLE #2: PRIDE IS PROBLEMATIC.
Humility is the opposite of pride, and it is pride that God detests. Humility is lowliness of mind that is appropriate for the creature before the Creator and the sinner before the holy God, so pride is the opposite of an appropriate attitude before God. Pride in the Hebrew means literally "a bubbling up or a foaming over." It is the attitude of self-exaltation at the expense of honoring God. Can you imagine anything more fundamentally wrong than exalting oneself as creature above the Creator? Can there be anything more inappropriate than sinners assuming that they know better than the Eternal One? Pride is offensive to God because it takes us from a place of cooperating in a divine plan to one of fighting both plan and Maker. Ultimately, it

seeks equality with God—the sin that transformed Lucifer from an angel to the devil.

Pride is also offensive to God because of its self-preoccupation. Pride regards self as fundamentally more significant than anybody else. When, many years ago, our eight-year-old son and his six-year-old sister indignantly complained to their mother that their four-year-old brother thought he was as important as they were, their reaction would have to be called pride. Pride is self-absorbed and denies what God decrees—that I should love God, and that I should love my neighbor as myself. C. S. Lewis wrote:

> In God you come up against something which is in
> every respect immeasurably superior to yourself. . . .
> A proud man is always looking down on things and
> people; and, of course, as long as you are looking down,
> you cannot see something that is above you.[49]

Pride also offends God because of its warped view of the self, which leads to self-delusion. There is no more deluded a person than the one who thinks creature is more important than Creator, sinner more significant than holy God, independence better than dependence, and disobedience more appropriate than obedience. Anybody who believes that fullness of life is found in self-absorption, rather than in service to God and to people, is utterly out of touch with the spiritual laws that God decreed before time and before human existence.

We should not be surprised that "the Lord detests all the proud of heart."

> The essential vice, the utmost evil is pride. Unchastity,
> anger, greed, drunkenness, and all that, are mere flea-
> bites in comparison: it was through pride that the devil
> became the devil: pride leads to every other vice: it is the
> complete anti-God state of mind.[50]

However, if we take seriously this business of pride, if we recognize it in our own hearts and come up with a right assessment of ourselves by humbling ourselves before the Lord, he promises that, ultimately, he will honor us.

Take the example of Solomon recorded for us in 1 Kings. Having succeeded David on the throne, he was aware that his father was a hard act to follow and that he had enormous responsibilities to fulfill. He was probably relieved when the Lord said to him, "Ask for whatever you want me to give you" (1 Kings 3:5). Wouldn't you like God to say that? Solomon's response is very illuminating:

> You have made your servant king in place of my father David. But I am only a little child and do not know how to carry out my duties. . . . So give your servant a discerning heart to govern your people and to distinguish between right and wrong. For who is able to govern this great people of yours?
>
> 1 KINGS 3:7, 9

There's a lot of humility in Solomon's response, and it was not wasted on the Lord. First he was humble enough to acknowledge God's grace. "You have made your servant king," he says. He did not say, "I am king because I deserve to be, because I've worked hard for it, and I am obviously the best choice for the job." He said, "I am king for no other reason than God graciously made me king."

Then, Solomon asked for "a discerning heart," so that he might govern the people properly. His response to the open-ended offer to ask for whatever he wanted was clear evidence that he was not in the business of exalting himself. He was eager to receive from God what he needed in order to serve the people. Not only that, but he also said, "I am only a little child and do not know how to carry out my duties"—a statement of his own inadequacy. Humility in Solomon's case is readily recognizable. He admits he owes everything to grace, he admits his own deficiencies, and he is willing to ask for help. As a result, God gives him what he asks for but also promises to honor him with great prosperity and success! Solomon is a great illustration of humility coming before honor.

The great Florentine preacher, Savonarola, on one occasion mentioned to a colleague that he'd been very impressed by an elderly lady who prayed fervently every day before a statue of the Virgin Mary. But Savonarola was disappointed when his colleague told him that there was nothing impressive about the woman's devotion. When she was young, she had been very beautiful and had served as the model for the statue. Every day since the statue's erection she had worshiped at its feet.

The ultimate sin is pride—a brand of self worship. It is fundamentally anti-God and anti-people, and that's why God detests it. If we are truly concerned with pleasing God, we must embrace this principle of humility, of seeing ourselves clearly in the light of God's word.

In contrast to the old woman of Florence, the story is told of Queen Victoria who, at the height of her powers as sovereign of the British Empire, used to attend a Bible study led by one of her servants—a footman. On one occasion the subject was the return of Christ, and the queen asked the footman when this might happen because she said that she could not wait to lay at Christ's feet the crown of the kingdom and empire. *That's* humility!

PRINCIPLE #3: SUBMISSION COMES BEFORE SUCCESS.

Recently I had lunch with my friends Jeremy and Heather. Jeremy was successful in business for many years before branching out into a new venture. Heather, who before marriage had been successful in the medical field, was thoroughly supportive and encouraging while raising four small children. I had followed their progress with interest and was eager to know how things were going for them. The report was that they had gone through three extremely difficult years, and their plans had not come to fruition as hoped, though their business was looking better than it had at any time. They also said that the things they had learned in the three years because of their adversity had been invaluable, and they honestly would not have traded their experience for three years' success in business. In their eyes, those three years of disappointing business had been a resounding success. The reason, they explained, was that they had learned about dimensions of life other than material success, which they would not have explored if the material success had come more quickly. Having known what it was to be successful *professionals*, they were getting around to being successful *persons*. And they liked what they were discovering.

Proverbs tells us:

> *To man belong the plans of the heart,*
> *but from the LORD comes the reply of the tongue.*
> *All a man's ways seem innocent to him,*
> *but motives are weighed by the LORD.*
> *Commit to the LORD whatever you do,*
> *and your plans will succeed.*

PROVERBS 16:1-3

We make our plans, which may or may not be the right ones. What determines whether or not they are correct is the motive behind them. We're not always clear on our motives, but God is, and he evaluates plans on the basis of motives. Therefore, we commit our plans and motives to the Lord and let him evaluate them. As we do, we can trust him to lead us in the right path—for the Lord works out everything according to his purposes.

So as I make plans, I say, "Here they are, Lord. To the best of my knowledge, my motives are right, but you test them and weigh them. I only want to do what pleases you. I commit my motives and my plans to you, and I ask you to change my heart, to work in my circumstances, to bring about your purposes. And I'll be certain of one thing—if I do that, as I submit to you, I know that you will make my life successful in your eyes."

Humility comes before honor, and submission before success. When we think about these two statements, we can't help but realize how far both are from common perceptions. We must decide if these are anywhere close to our own view of life. Am I motivated by humility and energized by submission? Do I have an overriding concern to please the Lord?

Avoiding What God Detests

> There are six things the LORD hates,
> seven that are detestable to him:
> haughty eyes,
> a lying tongue,
> hands that shed innocent blood,
> a heart that devises wicked schemes,
> feet that are quick to rush into evil,
> a false witness who pours out lies
> and a man who stirs up dissension among brothers.
>
> PROVERBS 6:16-19

The things listed here that God detests all have to do with social relationships. There are two words to describe these *detestable* attitudes and activities—"competitive" and "destructive." A case can be made for the benefits of healthy competition in sports and free enterprise, but there is nothing good to be said for the attitude that drives one to win at all cost, regardless of tactics used or damage done to others. When skill is pitted against skill so that both are sharpened by the experience, competition achieves something of value for all concerned. And where business competition results in better products at more reasonable prices, the merits of competition are obvious. But when competition degenerates into lies, cheating, violence, and psychological manipulation, this is detestable. Why? Because from God's point of view, whoever is being unfairly treated, violated, or destroyed is a person of infinite worth. That person, created in the divine image, has dignity and must not be degraded.

People love a winner. So does God, but he loves losers, too, like the "loser" who walks away from court bankrupted by the unethical practices of his competitors. Or the athlete limping away from opponents whose scheme succeeded. But surely he delights in those who, touched by the injury of the defeated, choose not to identify with the smirking "winners" but to reach out to the hurting losers, bringing comfort and restoring hope. It is not difficult to understand why God delights in the one and detests the other.

God also detests the kind of spiritual activity that is externally impressive but internally corrupted. For example:

> *The LORD detests the sacrifice of the wicked,*
> *but the prayer of the upright pleases him.*
> PROVERBS 15:8

> *If anyone turns a deaf ear to the law,*
> *even his prayers are detestable.*
> PROVERBS 28:9

The picture here is of somebody who engages in public worship activities, such as prayer and singing, but whose personal life is inconsistent with such activity. The worship experience, while purporting to be a reflection of the inner life, is in actuality a carefully crafted subterfuge. Others might be hoodwinked into believing that the religious person is indeed a person of spiritual integrity and devotion, but God knows that the religion is less than skin-deep and that the things he treasures are being callously abused to the hypocrite's advantage. This is detestable to the Lord.

So if we seriously desire to please the Lord, we should embrace what he decrees and avoid what he detests. He leaves us in no doubt that we should carefully weed out attitudes, social actions, and spiritual activities that he finds utterly distasteful.

Doing What God Desires

When I was a boy I tried to do what my parents wished—most of the time! I loved them, but I also knew there would be consequences if I disobeyed. Later in life when I joined the Royal Marines, I tried hard to do what my commanding officer ordered for similar reasons—I had no desire to become acquainted with the "brig," and also, less obviously, I respected him. When I married Jill, I wanted to do what she wanted me to do because I love her and want to make her happy. So for a variety of reasons throughout my life I have tried to do what I ought. But I have to admit that the greatest joy in doing what I ought has always been in bringing pleasure to the one for whom I was doing it.

Let me remind you of the verse with which we started this chapter:

When a man's ways are pleasing to the LORD,
he makes even his enemies live at peace with him.
PROVERBS 16:7

This is a remarkable assertion. The result of pleasing the Lord is a peace pact with the opposition. Remember that this proverb is a generally true principle, not a promise for each and every occasion. If I do things God's way, there is no doubt that my attitudes even toward my enemies will be extraordinary, and that being the case, it is likely that the opposition will eventually respond with more of a spirit of cooperation than competition.

But we should aim to please the Lord, whatever the consequences. He is pleased when we desire what he desires and do what he wishes. Here are three desires of God we can latch onto and practice in our lives.

DESIRE #1: GOD DESIRES THAT WE OBTAIN MERCY.
After stating, "The Lord detests all the proud of heart" and "They will not go unpunished," it is reassuring to read:

Through love and faithfulness sin is atoned for;
through the fear of the LORD a man avoids evil.
PROVERBS 16:6

The justice of God is married to the mercy of God. If God were less than just, it would spell chaos for the human race; if he were less than merciful, it would ensure disaster. Fortunately, through God's great love and faithfulness, he has satisfied his own justice in Christ's atonement, and he has extended his own mercy to the undeserving. God's great desire is that men, women, boys, and girls should avail themselves of the atoning work of Christ that brings forgiveness and reconciliation. Proverbs reminds us how:

He who conceals his sins does not prosper,
but whoever confesses and renounces them finds mercy.
PROVERBS 28:13

The Lord is delighted to give us mercy when we refuse to conceal our sins any longer and freely confess them. But so often we are reluctant to humble ourselves and admit to the Lord what kind of people we really are. The thought of contemplating our own sinfulness is too alarming, the idea of confessing too humiliating, and the thought of receiving mercy too undignified.

We become adept at concealment. We hide sin under pseudo-spirituality. We bury it under a pile of extenuating circumstances—we were victimized by circumstances or traumatized by environment. We put on an impressive display of benevolence and upright citizenship and trust that will be sufficient. But our natural constitution is reluctant to come clean. Our pride gets in the way, our self-sufficiency argues against mercy, and our self-righteousness questions our need for atonement.

All the time the Lord longs for us simply to stop concealing and start confessing. Nothing would please him more. David, the great psalmist, spoke dramatically about his own experience of "coming clean":

> *Blessed is he*
> *whose transgressions are forgiven,*
> *whose sins are covered.*
> *Blessed is the man*
> *whose sin the LORD does not count against him*
> *and in whose spirit is no deceit.*
> *When I kept silent,*
> *my bones wasted away*
> *through my groaning all day long.*
> *For day and night*
> *your hand was heavy upon me;*
> *my strength was sapped*
> *as in the heat of summer.*
> *Then I acknowledged my sin to you*
> *and did not cover up my iniquity.*
> *I said, "I will confess*
> *my transgressions to the LORD"—*
> *and you forgave*
> *the guilt of my sin.*
>
> PSALM 32:1-5

Augustine, the brilliant theologian whose previous life of debauchery had caused him such great sorrow, was desperately conscious of his need for forgiveness and never forgot the wonder of God's mercy. Psalm 32 was such a favorite of his that he had it written on the wall by his bed as he lay dying. Augustine's delight in forgiveness knew no limits even then.

The joys of the forgiver over the forgiven is unbounded. There are few things that bring more pleasure to God than forgiving us and showing us his mercy. This is what he desires.

DESIRE #2: GOD DESIRES THAT WE AVOID EVIL.

When evil wears the bloodstained garments of violence or the rags of starvation, it is not hard to recognize or difficult to reject. But when evil is garbed in the trappings of power or decked out in the finery of sensual gratification, it is much more difficult to avoid. But the Lord desires that we should avoid it. In the end, evil shakes its fist in the face of God and wrings the life from the heart of humanity. It may be attractive, but it will be destructive.

How can we best avoid the evils that appeal to us? By the "fear of the Lord." This means more than avoiding evil because we fear the Lord's indignation—although this aspect of the fear of the Lord should not be underestimated. But for the earnest believer, judgment—and avoiding it—is not the primary concern. Our stronger motivation should be that we are anxious not to displease him by succumbing to evil.

The ruthless tackle by a dirty athlete may cause lasting damage to a star performer, but when the star avoids the tackle with split-second reflexes and incredible coordination, he not only protects himself from danger, but he brings delight through his athleticism and grace. Evil is shown to be evil, and grace is shown to be graceful. The Lord delights in seeing us avoid the injury of evil, and he loves seeing us do it with grace and skill.

DESIRE #3: GOD DESIRES THAT WE ACT HONORABLY.

God always insists that the vertical relationship between himself and humankind be reflected in the horizontal dimension of person-to-person interaction. God is pleased not only by the way we relate to him, but also by the manner in which we respond to people. Proverbs reminds us:

The LORD detests men of perverse heart
but he delights in those whose ways are blameless.
PROVERBS 11:20

Blameless does not mean sinless or perfect, but it does signify the heart attitude of the person who wishes to live rightly before the Lord—the child who respects parents, the adolescent who is responsive to direction, the student who studies conscientiously without cheating, the employee who is reliable and trustworthy, the employer who is fair, the athlete who plays by the rules, the merchant who does business ethically, the husband and wife who are faithful, the politician who is honest, the attorney who seeks justice, the preacher who proclaims truth, the law officer who is compassionate, the civil servant who actually serves, and so on. There is nothing particularly "out of this world" about the lifestyle that pleases the Lord. It's a matter of living by divine rules in human society, of bathing the temporal in the glow of the eternal, and of touching the mundane with the marvelous. It wonderfully pleases the Lord, and it becomes increasingly pleasing to those who practice his values.

I remember reading about a woman who said that when she was a little girl all she wanted to do was please her daddy. Then he died. In adolescence she fell in love for the first time and all she wanted to do was please her boyfriend. Then he dumped her. Eventually she married and spent her time pleasing her husband, but he divorced her. So she devoted herself to her daughters in an effort to please them, but they married, left town, and she rarely heard from them. So she said, "I've spent all my life trying to please people and it never worked. So now I'm finally getting smart. I'm going to do what I should have been doing all along. I'm going to please myself."

Who cannot sense her despair and feel her pain? But with all due respect to this poor woman, she was wrong. She should not have been pleasing herself all along. She should have been pleasing the Lord. Then she would have known his pleasure.

AFTERWORD

All Scripture is inspired by God and is useful to teach us
what is true and to make us realize what is wrong in our lives.
It straightens us out and teaches us to do what is right. It is God's way
of preparing us in every way, fully equipped for every
good thing God wants us to do.
THE APOSTLE PAUL, 2 TIMOTHY 3:16-17, NLT

We have only skimmed the surface of the resources of the ancient book of Proverbs in our search for a system of values that can become the basis of sound and sensible decision making. This system is based on the character of the sovereign Lord and is to be reproduced in the lives of those who depend upon him and obey him through the Holy Spirit. I trust that we have seen enough to be stimulated, and to respond to what the Lord says to us about life. We need to hear it, those of us who live in a society being torn apart by competing values, where lives are being destroyed by actions based on wrong decisions.

Permit me to make a few suggestions.

1. Recognize the value of your Bible. It is God's Word. In it he reveals his person, his purposes, his promises, and his precepts. And he expects us to take them seriously. We recognize its value by reading it regularly, carefully, intelligently, and reverently.

    Regularly means we set aside some time every day—there are no written rules on how long to read the Scriptures—in the same way that we set aside time every day to eat material food.

    Carefully means we don't just skim the page, but we take time to thoughtfully consider what we have read. It will help if we take notes and keep them for further meditation.

    Intelligently means that we ask questions as we read and that we look for answers. We also use helpful books that will help us in understanding the Scriptures, and we talk to knowledgeable people about the things we have been reading, all the while praying that the Lord will give us understanding.

Reverently means that when we sit down to read, we realize that we are sitting at the feet of God, who is speaking to us himself. We listen to what he says, attentively and with awe.

2. Take time to pray about the things you are learning and the questions being raised in your reading of God's Word. Every relationship flourishes on communication and withers without it. Communication is a two-way street comprised of talking and listening. As we read Scripture, God talks to us and we listen. In prayer we talk to him and, incredibly, he listens. If you need a framework for prayer try this one:

P—praise—thank God for His goodness to you.

R—repent—talk to the Lord about the things that have been out of order in your life, seeking to turn from them and asking for his gracious forgiveness.

A—ask—bring your concerns and requests to the Lord on behalf of other people whom you know, knowing that he hears and answers in accordance with what is best for them.

Y—yourself—the tendency is to start here, but it is often better to leave your personal concerns until you have prayed about the other matters. It might be helpful to keep a list of people to pray for and the things about which you have prayed.

3. Make sure that you are worshiping regularly with other believers and spending time in biblical instruction in a church family. This will greatly assist you in your spiritual growth and development and present you with opportunities to develop your gifts in godly service to others.

4. Remember that the decisions you make in daily life should be based on the values that you have derived from God's Word, and avoid being drawn into the behavior of others whose lives are not built on God's principles.

5. Take time to care for other people, to share with them and to seek to be a source of blessing and encouragement to them.

6. In all things seek to bring the Lord delight.

NOTES

1. *Evolution: A theory in crisis* (Bethesda, Maryland: Adler and Adler, 1985).
2. *History of England*, vol.1, chap. 2.
3. (New York: Prentice Hall Press, 1991).
4. *Newsweek*, February 13, 1989.
5. "Why We'll Never Learn," *Newsweek*, July 23, 2001.
6. "Wall Street's New Honor Code," *Time*, June 25, 2001.
7. "The Myth of Value-Neutral Schooling," *Education Week*, November 7, 1984.
8. "How to Teach Right and Wrong," *Christianity Today*, December 13, 1993.
9. Ibid.
10. "Lewd Awakening," quoted in *Current Thoughts and Trends*, July 2001.
11. *Newsweek*, February 13, 1989.
12. *Newsweek*, June 8, 1992.
13. Hunter Lewis, *A Question of Values: Six Ways We Make the Personal Choices That Shape Our Lives* (San Francisco: Harper San Francisco, 1991).
14. Lewis, *A Question of Values*.
15. Louis Untermeyer, ed., *Modern British Poetry* (New York: Harcourt, Brace, and Howe, 1920). http://www.bartleby.com/103/. March 20, 2002.
16. *Religion in America* (The Brookings Institute, 1985), p. 344.
17. *The Australian*, June 13, 1992.
18. "Beliefs: General Religious" in Main Archives at Barna Research Online (http://www.barna.org). March 20, 2002.
19. *Walking in Wisdom* (Downers Grove: InterVarsity Press, 1983).
20. Vol. 5 (Grand Rapids: Zondervan, 1991).
21. Kenneth L. Woodward with Susan Miller, "What is Virtue?" *Newsweek*, June 13, 1994, pp. 38-39.
22. *Penseés*, IV, pp. 257, 220.
23. *People*, December 10, 1992, p. 89.
24. *Journal of the American Medical Association*, no. 15, p. 258.
25. (Anchor Books, 1969) 291.
26. *The Christian Mindset in a Secular Society* (Sisters, Oregon: Multnomah Press, 1984), p. 84.
27. Maris Vinovskis, "The Nuclear Family Goes Boom!" *Time*, October 15, 1992.
28. "The War against Women," March 28, 1994.
29. Op. cit.
30. "Garth Takes a Brave Stand," *Newsweek*, October 12, 1992.
31. *The Everlasting Man* (London: Hodder and Stoughton, 1934), pp. 3-4.
32. July 1989, p. 73.
33. "Dan Quayle Was Right", April 1993.
34. *The Body* (Dallas: Word, 1992).
35. *The Columbia World of Quotations.* (New York: Columbia University Press, 1996). http://www.bartleby.com/66/. March 20, 2002.
36. Joseph Daniel Unwin, "Sexual Regulations and Cultural Behavior," address

given on 27 March 1935, to the medical section of the British Psychological Society, printed by Oxford University Press (London, England).

37. D.J. Wiseman, ed. *Genesis,* Tyndale Old Testament Commentary. (London: The Tyndale Press,1967), p. 68.

38. (New York: Random House, 1981), p. 43.

39. James Patterson and Peter Kim, *The Day America Told the Truth* (New York: Prentice Hall, 1991).

40. *The Challenge of the Disciplined Life: Christian Reflections on Money, Sex, and Power* (San Francisco: Harper, 1989).

41. (New York: Harper and Row, 1985), p. 284.

42. Ibid., p. 303.

43. John Winthrop, *City upon a Hill,* p. 0.

44. "Lies, Lies, Lies," October 5, 1992, p. 37.

45. *A Little Treasury of American Poetry* (New York: Charles Scribner's Sons, 1952), p. 704.

46. Patterson and Kim, (New York: Prentice Hall Press, 1991).

47. *The Columbia World of Quotations.* (New York: Columbia University Press, 1996). www.bartleby.com/66/. March 20, 2002.

48. Robert Burns, "To a Louse."

49. *Mere Christianity* (New York: MacMillan, 1952).

50. Ibid.